THROUGH SEX
TO LOVE

THROUGH SEX TO LOVE

JOHN H. McGOEY, S.F.M.

Mary S. Lee

GALL PUBLICATIONS TORONTO

THROUGH SEX TO LOVE.

by John H. McGoey sfm.

First published in 1976 by Gall Publications.
Box 6666-A, Toronto, M5W 1X4.

ISBN: 88904 071 0.

Distributed by:

SAANNES Publications Ltd.
1293 Gerrard St. E.
TORONTO, CANADA. M4L 1Y8.

CONTENTS.

AUTHOR'S NOTE:

No one moves by MEANS OF, or FROM, sex to love. Past generations vainly tried to spiritualize human love by avoiding sex. The present generation immerses itself in sex only to find that it is without love. To be human is to be sexual by nature. Therefore, to love, one neither denies, nor avoids, nor gets bogged down in his sexual nature, but, in full acceptance of it, moves through the sexual to the personal dimension where love actually operates. Love then flows into every aspect of a relationship, including the sexual.

THROUGH SEX TO LOVE, says: Love is the power by which one understands and lives his sexual life well, or, love is all but impossible for anyone who misunderstands and mismanages his sexual life. One emerges as a mature person when he comes through sexual maturity to the point where love directs all his actions. Then he is a truly loving person in every sense of the word.

Preface: Through Sex to Love.

Years ago I undertook the celibate life as a priest and remain convinced that it is a fulfilling and rewarding one. Celibacy led to love and happiness for me. It seems clear that much of my happiness derived from understanding and accepting the basic principles of sex and love and their relationship to each other.

Like all celibate priests, on ordination I accepted the commitment to remain unmarried for life. Without knowing precisely how or why, I expected to find adequate compensation in my priestly life for the lack of a full genital life. I considered my "spiritual life" security enough against turning back or away from the priesthood. I chose the simplest form of discipline, a tight work schedule that minimized opportunities for exclusive personal relationships as well as the leisure for laziness or intrigue. Such relationships as I did have I monitored carefully and lived them from an upper level, as something like a friend but never quite an equal. I failed to see the arrogance of it, nor did I grasp how afraid I was of an equality in which I might not measure up.

Tensions that I refused to feel, and, that I seemed outwardly and consciously to carry well, eventually broke me. Circumstances then gave me the opportunity to do some of the thinking I had avoided, in the presence of people I loved and who loved me enough to tell me when and where they thought I was honestly mistaken, stupid, stubborn, or misguided. It was only during serious illness over several lengthy periods, when I had to accept close association and intimate care from women at their most compassionate and loving, that I could no longer escape reality. I was forced to measure celibacy for its meaning and rewards, against the need everyman has for a mate of his own, for life, in love.

I know that by the time I had to do my thinking, I had learned to think. By then, I knew that one's mind is apt to go out of gear in the uproar of the emotions, that maturity means the ability to think under the emotional impact of infatuation. It was my good fortune to have spent much time alone—in moments of truth, looking at the face of death when everyman is really alone; in war and under Communism in the isolation of China: in the tranquil peace of Harbour Island in the Bahamas; but, even more, in periods of misunderstanding, disapproval and some persecution. Out of this thoughtful solitude grew the conviction, which the years and subsequent experience have deepened, that it is love, not sex, that really matters. I realized that while people need each other desperately, true love is never born of desperation. It seemed that, in one sense, everyman *is* an island, because there is something lacking in the deepest personal union; there is a time in everyone's life when he must learn to live with himself before he can ever live happily with another, or others.

It is in solitude that man discovers what love really is, and whether he has the guts to really love. He sees lots of sex but very little love around him; the former is such an easy thing to do, the latter so difficult. He senses that to be fully human he has no alternative but to love, that love is a personal not a sexual thing, that the problem is that people do not really mean that much to one another.

As things are, with lots of help from the media and our culture, sex interferes terribly with man's loving. He blames his inhibitions and longs to be rid of them. He blames poor religious teaching and training and so disposes of real religion, his last ally in developing his capacity to love. Religion, after all, is man's response to or relationship with, first God, and then his fellow man. Yet if sex is the work of God it must be good. Religion teaches that, to be human, sex must be loving, not merely a way of procreation or self-indulgence. Many years of studied searching and thoughtful counselling have more than convinced me that sex apart from God and human loving simply does not work. It becomes merely another tool in man's personal pleasure kit. Such use is destructive of personal relationships. Only when understood and used well can sex find its real place in man's loving life.

A celibate priest can and must know as much about love as any married person. He can know a great deal about marriage, too, if he is interested in listening to the innumerable confused and disappointed married people who come to him wondering where love went, when in reality it never was. He need not be prejudiced in favour of marriage nor against it because of personal experience. He can be fairly detached, objective, and positive, one of the very few who can. He knows that for every priest who claims that he cannot hack life without a woman there are hundreds of married men who claim that they cannot hack life with one. He concludes that there are many people who will not hack life no matter how it is.

Herewith I present my ideas about sex and love for what they are worth. But one thing is certain. No one can be genuinely human unless he loves. Love is man at his very best, his happiest; love is the greatest human achievement.

John H. McGoey.

Introduction

There is very little wrong with the world which could not be solved by loving people. However, the emphasis today, in the developed world, is on sexual love, and much more on sex than on love. Yet only in man-woman, or married love is sex a prime factor. The mature person loves God, country, parents, children, brothers, sisters and neighbours – all loves in which the genital sexual factor is of secondary, if any, importance, despite the fact that the human person necessarily loves as a male or a female. Love is the great achievement of human life. If there must be a choice, it is more human to live without sex than to live without love. But, surely, to understand the more complex power to love one must first understand the simple function of sex.

Humanness comes only in male or female packages. Sex, which is male *and* female rather than male *or* female, is something which both share rather than that each has. Each person can experience only male or female sex; neither experiences singly what only both together can experience and understand. In fact, the opposite sex can be understood only vicariously, through communication. Yet each man and woman can love, can have personal wholeness in loving. The fullness of humanity is reached in the experience of deep personal love.

Marriage is the ordinary avenue to the fully loving life, since man's very existence depends on the genital sex function. His evolution and perfection, however, depend on the genital sex function integrated into the loving life. Nevertheless, single people and celibates are not deprived of the loving life because they choose not to use their genital sex function. Married people opt for love with a full genital sex life; single people opt for love without full genital function.

Love, single and married, requires the fullest possible understanding of sex. Sex, if not understood, or worse, misunderstood, as is more generally the case, makes loving all but impossible, is in fact as great an obstacle to love outside of marriage as in it. The poorest possible route to personal relationships is through the genitals. Human love is interpersonal rather than intersexual. A man's love for a man does not make him homosexual, nor does a woman's love for another woman make her lesbian. Yet one achieves human loving only as a sexual person. To achieve love one must have the basic knowledge of male and female anatomy and physiology, understand the sexual emotions and the relationship of sex to the spiritual dimension of man.

Love requires deep spirituality as well as full sexuality, integrated into the supreme power to love. Understanding both sexuality and spirituality is vital to love. Real people, mature people are essentially sexual, spiritual, understanding, but primarily loving. That is the message of this book.

That the writer is a celibate priest prompts the obvious question, "What does he know about marriage, sexual love expressed genitally, of which he admits no personal experience?" For one thing, he has been a full-grown man for a long time. He has spent many thoughtful years of living, has discussed life and love with many people of both sexes, all ages, several cultures, and numerous religious and areligious backgrounds. One need not have built an atomic bomb to drop one or to discuss intelligently the morality or consequences of doing so. One need not have a baby to be an obstetrician. One should know what he is talking about. If he does, it will make sense and work out well.

The writer has had considerable experience in personal relationships and loving and has discussed the loves and marriages of many others. What he has to say can stand on its own merit. If it is true people will be better, happier people for living it.

The material presented in the chapters "Sexual Anatomy" and "The Physiology of Sex" was prepared by E. Dawne Jubb M.D., F.R.C.S. (C) on staff at Women's College Hospital, Toronto, and an associate professor in the Department of Obstetrics and Gynaecology at the University of Toronto Medical School.

The drawings were done by an artist from the Medical Art Department of the Faculty of Medicine, University of Toronto, Toronto, Ontario, Canada.

Some of the material previously published for religious as *Dare I Love?* was supplemented by extensive revision and five totally new chapters for broader use and application.

CHAPTER ONE

Wholeness

Generations of philosophers were content to define man as a rational animal, heavily accenting the rational. Today, to explain man, naturalists (encouraged by a nearly perfect record of men making monkeys of themselves) capitalize on his remarkable resemblance to his closest living relative, the ape. Konrad Lorenz, the highly respected naturalist, said somewhat enigmatically, "Man is an animal, but he is essentially more than an animal." The simple truth seems to be that while man is no angel, neither is he an animal. He is in a class by himself. He certainly is not an ape who suddenly got smart. He is a unique being, a "human" being, with inherent powers to think and to love. Man's wholeness, his fulfilment, is reached in the development of these two powers. To be understood, *anything* man is must be related to *everything* he is—his entirety. Man is not simply of layer cake formation— animal plus an added layer to make him human. Rather he is human throughout; that is, every apparently animal quality in him is actually human.

To maintain his balance, man's power to love must keep pace with his power to learn. Man has concepts which he thoughtfully develops by relating them to prior concepts. He has fantastic ingenuity, despite the fact that at one time he understood thought as little as he still understands love. The institutions of higher learning everywhere testify to his progress in learning. But he also has the power to reflect, has the insight and understanding which precede love. He has the largely undeveloped power to equate the good of others with his own, which is what love does. Animal behaviour can shed some meagre light on the ways of man, but the human psyche is unique and few conclusions drawn from studies of animals can be applied validly to man. Certainly the power to love is strictly his own, and, when exercised, marks him as humanly whole.

Man is not well defined by fragmenting him into his various functions. He is said to have a spiritual life, a social and a sexual life, yet he really has one single, human life of many dimensions or aspects. Man's problems cannot be neatly isolated or localized. Whatever ails him, ails the whole person that he is. Professional religious life, as it has been, is a good example of the concentration on one dimension of man to the detriment of the whole person. The intense effort to spiritualize him did, in fact, dehumanize him. To grow spiritually man must grow humanly, personally, be more of a person, a better person. The holier the person the more truly human must he be. Spiritual imbalance makes people less human, whereas true holiness finds them saner, healthier, better developed, more knowing, and, above all, more loving people. The imbalance often seen in men of genius, artists and scientists, does not help them function better as people, to be more companionable, less islands in the sea of humanity.

The discipline of psychiatry is evidence enough that physical health does not make a whole man. Man's physical well-being is inextricably interwoven with his emotional and spiritual well-being. Abundant food and exercise are not enough to make man what he ought to be. He needs a true set of values and a high purpose to achieve fulfilment in depth. The most effective psychiatrists are those who believe that such values and motives, to a great extent, lead to the emotional and mental health and therefore to the general well-being of man. The good psychiatrist has a valid concept of the whole person and works toward the development of whole people.

The more impressive, though one-dimensional, are man's material achievements, the less satisfied he seems with his over-all life, the more doubtful about his personal role and identity. He is aware of a personal emptiness as he searches for deeper meaning in life than shelter, food, clothing and physical health. This awareness is a luxury far beyond people contending desperately with sickness, poverty, cold, hunger and discrimination. Affluent man is like the abandoned child adopted into a good home. Despite his relative comfort, he still wants to know who his parents are and why he was abandoned. Man wants to know where he came from and where he is going. He wants to know his relationship to whoever, or whatever, started it all. He knows that he lives and dies but he wants a reasonable explanation for doing so. He feels abandoned, disoriented when there is nothing bigger than himself in which to believe. His power to believe bothers him until he finds an object for it. The desire to look up to, and respect, interested and loving parents reflects his need for love, happiness, the secure continuity of the thread of love from God, through life, to God. Belief is a quality of the whole man. When man is deprived of belief, or deprives himself of it, he is exposed to every kind of superstition. He then believes in no one else, and is beset with doubts about himself, his role, the meaning of his personal life. Man may accept or reject it, but he needs a role, an identity, a purpose of his own. In these he can really live; he is whole.

There is no absolute wholeness for man, in the sense of perfection. His relative wholeness is indicated by the harmonious balance between his knowing and his loving, his search for the truth and his love of the good. He is most truly human and whole when he relates lovingly, thoughtfully and well to others, when he has a solidarity with them, when he belongs. He has then achieved his potential within human limitations. He is happy. Conversely, the unhappiness of a man, with or without power, wealth and pleasure, is evidence of his lack of wholeness, his state of unloving. Nothing brings man happiness; it originates within himself. Happiness cannot be legislated, precisely because it depends on good-will, and on man's power over the one person under his complete control, himself. Man can order all his faculties and functions to the happiness of the whole man. The addict, a disoriented man, is necessarily unhappy because of the anarchy in his life. His addiction, whatever it is, is bigger than he is. The happy man is immune to addiction.

Although many aspects of wholeness remain a mystery, the problems of mentally and emotionally ill people are abundantly clear. These are the people who do not relate to other people. Incapable of deeply loving relationships, they are sick, crippled, part people. The physical cripple is the more obvious, but he can and does manage far better than the emotional cripple. Emotional cripples are seldom or easily recognized, and they themselves rarely suspect their condition before it is fully developed, or have the courage to face it when they do suspect it. One is completely horrified by a trip to a veterans' hospital where the broken bodies, the human remnants left in war's wake, can be seen. The frightful cost of war is immediately and shockingly evident. However, the emotional cripples surfacing everywhere today in the affluent society are not the result of war but of the human irresponsibility and unloving, which these days are equated with "peaceful" living. They are cripples simply because they have been deprived of the love needed to inspire them to love others, to grow humanly. No wonder drug or miracle of science touches them; there is no synthetic substitute for love. Unhappy, they substitute pleasure for love and become pleasure's addicts. Even love cannot cure those too damaged to appreciate it, or too rejected to believe in it. They have but the slightest hope of ever living. Genetics cannot eliminate them; birth control or abortion cannot forestall them; suicide is a relief for them. Birth of loving people into loving families, life in a loving and concerned society, is the only answer. The greatest need in society today is for whole people to provide this loving milieu.

History amply indicates that education of itself has never enabled man to act well, to be happy. Certainly the problems of educated man are more complex than those of simpler people. Regardless of the number of solutions it provides for physical, spiritual, economic or social problems, learning hardly touches the problem of man himself. His basic personal problem is the neglect of his power to love. Learning brightens man's mind but loving warms his heart, and his survival requires warmth as much as light. The brightest man in the world is not whole until he loves. Love saves the brightest minds from being caught up in material trivialities which smother them. The ruthless exploitation of one man by another is the incredible price of unloving. Personal and political corruption, the rackets, addictions, greed and tyranny of every kind result from unloving.

Man has fallen just short of believing that education could make him a god. Many bright men once thought it possible to accumulate all knowledge. Now, the more a man learns the clearer it becomes how much he has yet to learn. As Sir Bernard Lovell said so well, "Each new scientific discovery of man makes it clear how much farther he is from where he thought he was." Currently, man discovers problems faster than he can identify them let alone solve them. He is like the man patching an old inner tube—as soon as one hole is patched, another blows open. Man must now bring his power to love up to the level of his power to learn. He must understand the fantastic difference between sex and love, and their relationship to the process of personal growth. This process requires him to examine sex, which is so involved in human loving that many mistakenly identify them.

Perhaps there was a time when love was not so important for the survival of the human race. That day is gone. Affluent civilization has reached the point where loving is indispensable to real progress; is, in fact, the difference between real and imagined progress. A theology of poverty and suffering brought the race through its birth pangs; a theology of affluence and sharing can bring it to maturity. Love is sharing, having the wherewithal to share wholeness. It is not enough for man to research sex, he must also study human love in depth so that he will be able to understand, teach, learn and live it. He can no longer afford the easy delusion that sex is love, or that love necessarily has any real connection with genital sex. The evolution of man may well depend on love, to make room in the world for living. The unacceptable alternative is the human jungle, teeming with emotional cripples, cannibalizing each other for survival.

CHAPTER TWO

Sex and Sexuality

The terms sex and sexuality are often used interchangeably. In this book a distinction is made. The term sex generally refers to the genital function; sexuality refers to the quality of maleness or femaleness pervading the whole personality. Sexuality is the inescapable fact of living, from birth to death, as male or female. It is the polarity between male and female, in the physical, physiological, psychological, spiritual and personal human dimensions. One is inescapably male or female in everything one thinks or says or does. The failure to differentiate between the genital function, which one may or may not use, and the inevitable fact of human sexuality with which one lives twenty-four hours a day, is unfortunate. On one hand, this failure has made the necessary genital sexual control seem to demand suppression of the sexual emotions; and on the other hand, the inescapable sexuality has seemed to make genital sex compulsory.

The sexual function is inseparable from the genital organs but not restricted to them. It involves the whole person. Certainly, the most obvious thing about people is their maleness or femaleness. Sexuality is most evident in the genital function but diffuses itself through the whole spectrum of human relations. It expresses itself in all the physical, emotional, mental and spiritual factors and attitudes that can be identified as male and female. People still remain male and female when the genital function has long ceased. Furthermore, sexuality is so related to loving (although it is not to be identified with it) that no human form of affection or love can be expressed other than as male or female. Both compassion for an afflicted fellowman, and love for God Himself, can be expressed only in the way of a man or a woman.

The Judeo-Christian heritage carried with it some contempt for man's undoubted physical relationship to the animal. The things of the mind, spirit and immortal life were stressed almost to the exclusion of the things of the emotions, body and mortal life. The "flesh" was begrudgingly tolerated as "lower nature". Continuing reference to the warring of the spirit against the flesh, and the flesh against the spirit, all but split man's personality, and helped little to reconcile these inseparable parts of man to his essential unity. Bodily functions were ignored if possible, sex was unmentionable, and sexuality considered animal, while the glories of the mind were sung without restraint. Certainly the idea of being first cousin to an ape shocked the Victorian much more than the scandal of evil in man's personal life. This nearly successful repudiation of human sexuality, and the refusal to discuss sex with the tolerance required for understanding any vital function, created the atmosphere for the sexual permissiveness which now exists.

There is great pressure on contemporary man to face and accept his sexuality as fully as he does his intellectuality. Such acceptance will permit the genital function to find its rightful place, and allow its real limitations to be established. The normal role of sex in serving rather than dominating interpersonal relationships would then be determined by true love rather than dictated by sexual passions. Thus, either the use of genital sex or abstaining from it could be recognized as equally loving. It is precisely when love governs the actions of man that sexual pleasure finds its correct place in the ordered life of the happy man or woman, single or married.

Personal happiness determines the role of sex, eliminating the unnecessary sexual frustration so prevalent in both courtship and marriage. Clearly sex is as vital to single happiness as it is to the happiness of the married person. There is never a need to exaggerate or minimize the importance of sex in the lives of the loving. Genital sex, misunderstood or mismanaged, is as destructive of love in marriage as outside of it, because it dominates, or obscures, the person of the loving or the loved.

Knowledge of both genital sex and sexuality, like all knowledge, comes through the senses. The anatomy and physiology of sex, while admittedly the mere beginning of the sex education so basic to understanding sex and love, must be completely familiar and precisely known. To this end the next two chapters of this book are directed. Though they may be superfluous for some readers, the knowledge they contain is indispensable to understanding subsequent things which are not nearly as obvious.

CHAPTER THREE

Sexual Anatomy

Sex is the material of chastity, both single and married. Ignorance of sex by those in either state is equally deplorable. Some choose to forgo for life the full genital function; married people choose to live a full sexual life. It is inexcusable that anyone be encouraged or allowed to undertake either way of life without a thorough knowledge and understanding of sex. Such knowledge must include both male and female sexual anatomy.

Confrontation with their sexual organs comes earlier and easier to boys than to girls, for from infancy they have handled these organs each time they have gone to the bathroom. Girls require a more studied recognition of their sexual organs, which are normally invisible to them. For females, until recently, ignorance of their sex organs has frequently been considered a virtue.

Reference to the male and female genitals by the common use of vulgar terms originated in ignorance of the correct terminology for the organs, and in religious and cultural denigration of things sexual. This is generally avoided when parents and teachers use the correct names for sex organs in speaking even to the youngest children. The easy use of the right names makes possible the open and intelligent discussion of sex and its functions required for proper development and maturity, and removes much of the superficial mystery from the subject.

Curiosity about sex is in no way morbid but quite normal and healthy. In the best interests of all, it should be satisfied, as all genuine intellectual curiosity should be, with correct, factual information.

The pictures accompanying this chapter could conceivably cause some emotional turmoil in one unfamiliar with the material. However, nothing should excuse the detailed study and understanding of these pictures. The measure of the upset is clear evidence of the need for the knowledge available through them.

MALE GENITAL ANATOMY.

Penis

Cylindrical organ composed of erectile tissue and covered with loose, hairless skin. It is traversed longitudinally by a central canal, the urethra, which serves to transport the urine from the bladder, mucous lubricant from Cowper's glands, and semen from the seminal vesicles to the exterior. The resting state of the organ is flaccid and freely mobile (spongy erectile tissue is empty and soft), and approximately 4¼ inches in length. In the erect state, spongy tissue is filled completely with blood, causing penis to be rigid in a stationary position, with its long axis running upward and outward at an angle of about 45 degrees from the anterior abdominal wall. The erect penis is about 1½ inches in diameter and 6-7 inches long.

Glans Penis

Very sensitive cap on the outer end of the penis, also traversed by the urethra.

Prepuce (foreskin)

Fold of very loose, wrinkled, hairless skin surrounding the glans penis, but not attached to it. Circumcision is the operation removing this fold of skin.

Scrotum

Sac of hairy skin attached below and behind the penis, containing the two testicles.

Testicle

Male sex gland which produces the germ cells (spermatozoa) and the male sex hormone, testosterone.

Seminal Vesicle

Sac interiorly situated behind and below the bladder, for storage of spermatozoa.

Prostate Gland

Large gland at base of bladder which secretes fluid and mucus in which sperm are carried to the outside during ejaculation.

Cowper's Gland

Tiny mucus-secreting gland below prostate which discharges mucus into urethra to pass through the glans penis to act as lubricant for intercourse.

Littre's Glands

A series of small mucus-secreting glands opening individually into the penile urethra.

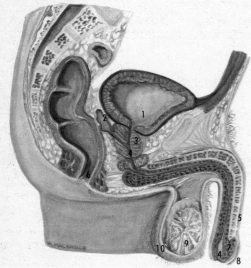

1. bladder
2. seminal vesicle
3. prostate gland
4. urethra
5. penis
6. anus
7. glans
8. prepuce (foreskin)
9. testicles
10. scrotum

Figure A

FEMALE GENITAL ANATOMY.

Vulva
External female genital organs, that is, all that is visible in Figure C.

Labia Majora
Two folds of hairy skin, covering fatty tissue.

Labia Minora
Two thin folds of mucous membrane (soft, moist tissue) next to the inside borders of the labia majora, which meet anteriorly to cover the clitoris like a hood. Deep under these thin folds are two masses of erectile tissue called the vestibular bulbs.

Clitoris
Analogue or equivalent of the male penis; cylindrical organ of erectile tissue approximately one inch long and ¼ inch in diameter, covered by the anterior part of the labia minora.

Glans Clitoris
Very sensitive cap on the end of the clitoris.

Hymen
An incomplete membrane of thin mucous, elastic tissue, extending from the base of one of the labia minora to the base of the other, across the entrance to the vagina. The opening in the centre is of varying sizes. The hymen is often not elastic enough to allow sufficient stretching without tearing, to accommodate the erect penis at first intercourse, and occasionally it is so rigid as to prevent completely the entrance of the penis. Hymenectomy is the name of the operation to enlarge the opening through the hymen into the vagina.

Bartholin's Glands
Small glands situated deep in the tissues beneath the posterior end of the labia minora. They produce mucus which is deposited near the opening into the vagina at its posterior end, to act as a lubricant during intercourse.

Skene's Glands

Tiny glands in the tissue about the urethra which produce mucus deposited at the opening of the vagina at its anterior end, also acting as lubricant during intercourse.

Vagina

Hollow tube of soft muscular tissue attached to the cervix above (inside), and continuous with the vulva below (outside). Its resting state is collapsed with front and back walls of tube touching. The front wall is approximately 3½ inches long, the back wall approximately 5 inches long. The vagina's diameter is very variable; it is narrowest at rest, widest (at least 4 inches) during delivery of a baby. The direction of the canal, about 45 degrees from the horizontal, extending back and upwards when standing, matches the angle of the erect penis.

Uterus (womb)

A hollow, pear-shaped organ with very muscular walls. Lower end is called the cervix (neck of the womb) and protrudes slightly into the vagina. The lining of the uterine cavity, the endometrium, is very responsive to variations in sex-related hormone levels; it is the tissue in which a fertilized ovum (egg cell) implants, and from which it gets its support at the beginning of a pregnancy. This same lining becomes the menstrual flow when it is sloughed off and drains through the vaginal opening each month that no pregnancy takes place.

Fallopian Tubes

Two muscular tubes extending from the sides of the top of the uterus, sideways, and out to the ovaries. Their length is about 4-4½ inches, diameter about ¼". The tube transports egg cells from the ovary to the cavity of the uterus.

Ovary

Female sex gland, almond-shaped, 1½ x 1 x ½ inches in size. It houses immature female germ cells called ova and produces female sex hormones, oestrogen and progesterone.

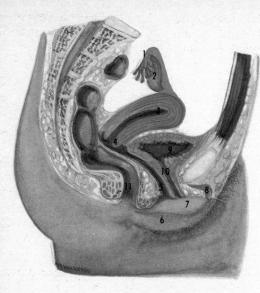

1. fallopian tube
2. ovary
3. uterus
4. cervix
5. vagina
6. labium majus
   (outer lip)
7. labium minus
   (inner lip)
8. clitoris
9. bladder
10. urethra
11. anus

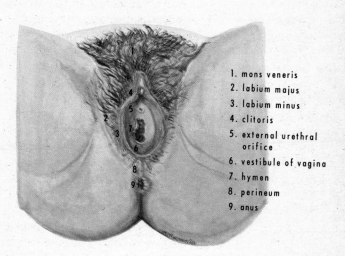

1. mons veneris
2. labium majus
3. labium minus
4. clitoris
5. external urethral
   orifice
6. vestibule of vagina
7. hymen
8. perineum
9. anus

Figure C

CHAPTER FOUR

The Physiology of Sex

As anatomy describes the appearance of the organs of sex, physiology describes their function. The sex of a person is decided at the time of conception. Like the bone structure, the skin colouring, etc., the sex comes from the pooling of the chromosomes from the mature male and female germ cells, the sperm and the ovum.

During the first eight weeks of intrauterine life, the sex of the foetus can be discovered only by the examination of the chromosome makeup of individual cells. By the eighth week the appropriate gonad (sex gland, ovary or testis) is differentiated. By the twelfth week all the sex organs are present in the foetus.

From the twelfth week of intrauterine life to the age of puberty the genital organs remain in an infantile stage, increasing in size as the body grows but not maturing. During this stage, the external sex organs can respond to local, mechanical stimuli in an infantile form of arousal and orgasm response, and often do.

At puberty, the master gland of the body, the pituitary gland, which is located deep in the skull at the base of the brain, initiates stimulation of the sex glands (testes or ovaries) by means of hormones called gonadotrophins. Stimulation of the sex glands results in two basic developments: (i) an increase in the output of the appropriate sex hormones; (ii) maturation of the germ cells in the gonad.

The main male sex hormone secreted by the testes is testosterone. Under the influence of this hormone there is rapid growth and development of the male sex organs at puberty, and their maintenance throughout the life of the man. This hormone also brings out the secondary sex characteristics. Hair over the whole body becomes coarser and more abundant, especially in the armpits, genital region and beard. The larynx enlarges, increasing resonance and deepening the voice. The general body build develops, musculature and athletic inclinations increase.

In the testes the immature germ cells—the spermatagonia—become mature male germ cells—spermatozoa—each complete with a tail for motility, and carrying in its nucleus the particular genetic material this male can contribute to a new person. The mature male germ cells are stored and nourished in the seminal vesicles behind and beneath the bladder.

The main female sex hormone is oestrogen. Under its influence, at puberty, the female genital organs grow and mature rapidly. The labia majora (outer and larger lips) grow large enough to conceal the labia minora (inner and smaller lips). The vagina grows in length, diameter and rugosity, and the ovaries, uterus and tubes increase in size. The female secondary sex characteristics become apparent. The breasts develop, first as buds, deep to the nipples, and then with more generalized enlargement. Hair appears in the genital region and in the armpits. Fat depositions occur predominantly in the mons veneris (lower abdomen covering the front of the pelvic bone), but also over the buttocks and thighs. The general body build becomes one of soft contours, broad hips, large thighs and a relaxed musculature.

In the ovary itself, maturation of the primitive female germ cells begins. However, unlike the maturation of the male germ cells (sperm), which is continuous, with mature sperm being stored in the seminal vesicles in huge numbers, in the female only one ovum matures each month, and no mature ova are stored. As soon as the ovum is mature it is extruded from the ovary (ovulation), and it is then propelled through one of the uterine tubes to the uterine cavity. A mature ovum lives only about twenty-four hours after ovulation unless it is penetrated by a viable sperm (conception). If this does not occur, the ovum dies and passes out through the uterus, cervix and vagina. Simultaneously with the ovarian maturation and extrusion process of the ovum, and resulting from hormone stimulation directly related to it, the lining of the uterine cavity (the endometrium) becomes very thick and lush in readiness to supply nutrition and support for the fertilized ovum, should conception take place. Each month without conception, the ovum dies, the endometrial lining becomes superfluous and is sloughed off (menstruation). It is the fragments of this lining and the small amount of blood extruded with it which constitute the menstrual flow.

Once the genital organs have reached a mature state, shortly after the onset of puberty, they are *fully* capable of performing the sexual act. Sexual intercourse, or coitus, takes place when the erect penis is fully accepted by the receptive vagina, where mutually stimulative interaction induces the male and female orgasm or climax. The sexual response or orgasm, spontaneous or induced, can take place in either male or female alone. When it occurs as a result of mechanical stimulation apart from intercourse it is called masturbation.

The genital sexual activity in each sex begins with a local genital lubrication. In the male, a small amount of mucus appears at the tip of the penis. This is not semen, but mucus from the Cowper's glands, and some small (Littre's) glands along the penile portion of the male urethra. Its purpose is to lubricate the tip of the penis to facilitate its entry into the vagina. In the female, at an early stage of the sexual response, the Bartholin and Skene glands near the opening of the vagina secrete mucus for lubrication at the entrance to the vagina. The vaginal walls themselves also secrete mucus to facilitate movement of the penis in the vagina during intercourse.

The second stage of sexual response is one of excitement or arousal. There is a generalized increase of the blood content of the genital organs and the breasts of both sexes. The arterial blood supply to the spongy erectile tissues is markedly and suddenly increased, while the venous exit for the blood is simultaneously slowed, so that the tissue involved becomes stuffed with blood, firm and pulsating. The male penis becomes rigid and elongated like a thick rod, in a stationary position with its long axis running upward and outward from the front of the body. At the same time the scrotum becomes flattened and elevated, the testes are pulled higher in the sac and become larger, the male nipples erect. In the female, the glans of the clitoris swells and the clitoral shaft increases in diameter. The erectile tissue, deep to the labia minora, fills with blood, the labia minora swell up and spread the labia majora in preparation for the entry of the penis. The uterus and cervix enlarge somewhat, are pulled up and back in the pelvis, lengthening the vagina. The vaginal walls become a barrel-like tube increasing in length and diameter. The walls of the outer third of the vagina become more swollen with blood than the rest of the vagina walls, narrowing this part of the vagina like a thick cuff, which grips the penis when it is present. The female breasts enlarge generally and the nipples erect.

When the climax or orgasm is reached a series of rhythmic contractions takes place at intervals of approximately four-fifths of a second, in all the erectile tissue of both sexes. The main feature of the female orgasm is the rhythmic contractions in the outer third of the vaginal barrel and the other engorged tissue surrounding it, including the clitoris. The uterus and cervix also contract at the same rate. The main feature of the male orgasm is a series of rhythmic contractions of the penis matching the vaginal contractions. Similar contractions occur in the seminal vesicles and the prostate gland. These organs expel their contents, which together form the semen, into the urethra where the penile contractions ejaculate it from the penis, with sufficient force to shoot it two feet beyond the end of the penis if it is not contained.

These events in the male and female are accompanied by other body changes. Pulse rate, blood pressure and respiration increase sharply. Most muscle groups in the body go into spasm, hands and feet tense, face contorts, sphincters clamp shut, a rash may appear, and there is often marked sweating.

Following orgasm there is a release of muscle tensions throughout the body, and a release of blood from the engorged areas. The most obvious change in the male is the prompt loss of erection, and the shrinkage of the penis to its normal, unstimulated size. The breast swelling of the female disappears first, then the clitoris and other areas of erectile tissue revert to their usual size.

Physiologically these basic patterns of bodily function remain the same for all intercourse, but psychologically the experiences may feel and be altogether different depending on many circumstances. Sexual intercourse may be an act of deep personal love undertaken in the hope of conceiving a child of that love. It may be a casual visit to a prostitute, or a highly charged, emotionally dominated and irresistible act of passion or lust. These aspects are beyond mere physiology.

The primary purpose of the genital organs, of course, is the production of human beings, the preservation of the species. It is a function vital to the human race but in no way vital to the individual person. It is a voluntary function, and each individual can decide at any time whether he or she wishes to proceed with a genital sexual response or not. That control, which is in every human being, in potential at least, is the basis for responsible parenthood, required not only for conception and birth but more vitally for the proper rearing of children.

The normal state of the genital organs is at rest. Some stimulation is required for their function as genitals. The stimulation can be local, general, physical or psychological. If simple touching of these organs alone were sufficient to stimulate them, they would be automatically stimulated by the clothing, or by the handling for bathing or elimination processes. The usual initiating stimuli are psychic, and dependent on sexual polarity even in autoeroticism. Ideally the reponse should be elicited by a genuinely loving relationship and carried to completion only in a marriage which is responsible, enduring and securing. Man has that potential, and is most fully human when exercising it.

CHAPTER FIVE

The Sexual Emotions

It is certainly easier to describe than to define the emotions. They register the impact of experience much as the eye registers a picture. They are like inner senses, receiving material from the outer senses, adding the reactions experienced, filtering everything through to the mind for processing into practical judgments. The emotions transfer the outside world to the mind; they connect the flesh to the spirit, trigger the intellect. Stimulated by the emotions, the mind moves into gear. Good judgment requires a well-working set of emotions to supply the material of judgment. The emotions are man's thermostatic controls of pleasure and pain. Through them he comes close enough to the fire to get warm and stays far enough away to avoid being burned, comes close enough to people to be appreciated and stays far enough away to avoid rejection. The emotionally mature man is the one who can enjoy all the pleasure that is good for him and accept none that is harmful, who can accept all the pain that is beneficial to him and reject all that is unnecessary. For such a person pleasure registers as pleasure and pain registers as pain, but he is not dominated by these feelings. The emotions are meant to serve the whole person; they are in no way supposed to run one's life. It is essential to live with one's emotions, not without them, and to have an awareness of one's feelings in general, so that one can identify them specifically. The latter ability indicates a high state of emotional health. One should always experience the feelings normally expected in any given situation. When this is not so, emotional problems of one kind or another are present.

No secondary function of man plays a more important role in his development than do the emotions. They function very much like the amber traffic light, warning of a changing situation to be met. There would be utter chaos at a busy urban intersection if there were not some warning between the red and green lights controlling traffic. The drivers of the cars approaching the intersection from all directions require time to make the proper judgment for passing safely through, or stopping to avoid collision. The amber light provides that time and alerts one to caution, vigilance. The driver then makes the considered judgment to continue or to stop gradually, gently enough to avoid being hit from the rear or dangerously jolting his passengers. The eye registers the amber light; its meaning or impact is registered by the emotions, and the mind makes the judgment about the action to be taken.

The proper role of the emotions is in the order: I feel, I think, I act; *e.g.*, I feel angry, I decide on a beneficial course of action, I carry it out. The emotionally troubled or crippled person short-circuits this procedure into: I feel, I act, with generally unhappy results; *e.g.*, I feel angry, I pick up a knife and stab my adversary. The emotions simply are not built or equipped to do the work of the mind, to make judgments.

Emotional problems are inevitable when anyone permits the feelings to dominate judgment, acting on impulse rather than after due consideration of the situation presented. (Trained reflex actions are not to be considered impulsive.) For example, on meeting a lion face to face one man faints, another screams, another freezes so rigidly the lion might break his teeth on him, while still another, getting the full implications of the situation as his feelings rush upon him, very gently but efficiently reaches for his gun and shoots the animal. Only in the last case did the man use the emotions. In the other cases the persons were completely dominated by their emotions—either negatively, completely withdrawing from reality, or positively, taking a rash and quite unwarranted action. The proper use of the emotions enables one to see and understand a situation as it really is, make the right judgment, and so meet the situation wisely.

Something happens which one sees, hears or senses in some way. One reacts. One feels anxious, elated, threatened, depressed, resentful, angry, disgusted, sad, pleased, joyful, hopeful, encouraged, and so on. Man experiences, or ought to experience, a full spectrum of emotions or reactions to each life situation, according to its nature. None of these feelings is in itself good or bad. It is merely important that it get through, register correctly, present the right information. The earlier and more clearly the message comes through, the more time and calm is provided for working out the right decision and the appropriate action.

The teacher, for example, depends to an extreme on her properly operating emotions, for the handling of her class. Children quite typically take the measure of the teacher, very early—will she run them or will they run her? A child sets out to challenge the teacher, to irritate her. Made aware of the challenge, the teacher reacts with a slow burn (called burn because it is felt), she gets hot under the collar. This reaction, amber light, tips her off to the direction of her reaction to the happening, that she is verging on anger. The warning leads her to handle the situation correctly for the best interest of the child, the class, and her own poise and effectiveness. She has the power to cool it, to simmer down. She needs no more reaction; she got the message. What is required now is thought—how to handle the situation? She uses her wisdom and experience to avoid lashing out at the child, which would be precipitate, unfair, probably both unhappy and wasted. Her over-reaction would only set off another, there would be a complete impasse and polarization of sympathies, an unnecessary confrontation. The good teacher's emotions are recognized and used long before they reach hurricane force. They serve their purpose well by prodding the mind to provide a prudent and wise solution to the problem presented. Teachers who overreact, and those who allow themselves to be threatened or intimidated, are all emotionally dominated, and can only handle such situations badly.

There is no choice connected with the emotions, no freedom. They are mechanical, automatic, infallible indicators of the situation presenting itself for management. The emotions cannot tell lies, but they can be interfered with by the master power of the person, who can suppress them or insist on taking the wrong message from them. However, their abuse is always a mistake. Every emotion is a very identifiable feeling with its proper name, expressing a specific, normal reaction to a situation to which it points as surely as a compass needle. If read correctly, it indicates the nature of the situation with which one is presented. The rule for the emotions is: never suppress them, never exploit them, always express them; that is, permit them to be felt, so that they can be recognized and used in the relationships one must have with other people and other things. Everyone else does not have to know how I feel, but I must know, so that I can be aware of the situation as it truly is, and so make judgments about it as demanded by truth and love.

Many people handle their emotions badly because it has been all but accepted over the years that the emotions were the problem rather than infallible indicators of the solution. When someone was described as "emotional" it seemed more an accusation than a statement of fact. Man is essentially emotional and would be hopelessly handicapped otherwise. Unfortunately the term was applied to those who vented their emotions on others, abused them rather than used them for their own insight and personal understanding. It was a social sin to express one's emotions and a virtue to suppress them in the name of the famous "stiff upper lip" of good behaviour. Those who think of emotions as bad, or accept the stupidity that "one must rise above one's feelings" by suppressing them, actually never allow these feelings to register, and so have to be out of touch with the true situations around themselves. The emotional reactions of such people often register on those standing around them, without being felt by the persons whose emotions they are. Those who suppress their feelings are bland, colourless, and deep-frozen to protect themselves from pain, even the most necessary and helpful. People who exploit their emotions, that is, wallow in them and are carried away by them, are social menaces and incapable of relating to others in a responsible way.

The clear messages of the emotions are always rejected by people for whom the truth is bad news. They cannot or will not face real situations, and the rejected messages from their emotions usually result in various psychosomatic illnesses. When permitted to dominate, positively or negatively, abused emotions can lead to addictions of every kind, to tension, confusion and such depression that there is often complete inability to cope with even the minor realities of life. The alcoholic, for whom the bottle is bigger than the man, the fat slob addicted to the refrigerator, trying vainly to fill an empty life with food, the drug addict whose idea of "precious" is the little pill or the hypodermic needle which carries him to the never-never land, the sex addict for whom copulation is love, are all emotional cop-outs.

Certainly, real human relationships of any kind are beyond the emotionally suppressed, unfeeling person. Obviously a healthy emotional life is vital for anyone hoping to achieve a true loving relationship. Since emotions are the inner eyes of man, it is hard to understand why one who does not despise his eyes could be disdainful or frightened of his feelings. It is silly for a man to refuse pain, however useful or necessary, or to embrace pleasure however harmful or destructive, but that is precisely what is done when the emotions are ignored or mismanaged. The depressed person will register nothing which is happy or joyful, the elated person will register nothing which burdens or obligates.

The high incidence of emotional illness today is due both to better understanding (and so greater fear of the havoc wrought by abuse of the emotions) and the vastly increased emotional pressure of current living, and the inability of people to meet that pressure. In times past there was much more general tranquillity and a much slower pace to life. Healthy emotions today must be like highly sensitive radar. A few years ago the eyes and the foghorns were enough to take care of ships in the fog. Ships were fewer, travelled more slowly, and were so constructed as to give without disintegrating on impact. However in the space age there are new requirements. A keener eye is needed to sense objects through fog and in darkness. Radar was cleverly invented and devised, a supersensitivity to what could not be seen. The naked eye cannot directly handle air traffic, even on the clearest day, when hundreds of huge craft hurtling through space depend on human judgment to land and take off without accident. The more sensitive the radar the more time and wider margin for safe decision is possible. The emotions are the radar of human behaviour and now need to be more sensitive than ever to make right judgment possible in the complicated human relations of modern society.

The emotions must be seen as tremendous assets, never as liabilities. The higher the evaluation of them, the more quickly and gladly is recognized the role they must play and their tragic mismanagement will be much less. Through their wizard use the successful salesman sizes up his prospect with real insight and tailors his pitch to him. The same correct use of them is equally effective in all human relationships. Through them comes the insight to appreciate the positions of others, to understand and compassion-ate them, to know a friend from an enemy, to cement the bond of friendship and reconcile oneself to an enemy. They enable a man to handle himself well in most situations and to bring harmony from most discords. Nowhere are they more vital than in loving. Through reading them correctly true values are discovered in the loved one, understanding is made possible, and love endures. It is the emotions which double a joy and halve a sorrow shared. It is through them that one approaches his friends in love in the first place. They are indispensable both in the approach to long-lasting, loving relationships and wise and happy marriages, and in avoid-ing seduction through impossible relationships with incompatible people. The emotions, badly understood and miserably managed, have broken up more possible love relationships, more meetings of minds and councils of the wise than most other factors. Handled well, they give the feel of coming events and usher them gently into the arena of reason where they are worked out satisfactorily.

The dictionary's use of the words "think" and "feel" inter-changeably reflects very well the tendency of the emotions to usurp by default the place and work of the mind. Although the emotional centres are in the brain, the emotions must never be confused with the mind. Their functions are poles apart, though the emotions are handmaid to the mind. It is a mistake to identify what one feels about something with what one thinks about it. All knowledge coming through the senses is filtered through the emo-tions to the cerebral cortex which does the computing, the think-ing. The rampant emotions play havoc with the data processing of the mind: the deep-frozen emotions, which do not process infor-mation, deprive the mind of the material for its work.

When the mind, whose object is the truth, betrays its trust, as it does when it rationalizes invalid foregone conclusions, it rejects the painful truth or accepts the pleasant lie by suppressing or ex-ploiting the emotions, which normally express the situation to the mind as it really is. Nothing so impedes the pursuit of truth as the blocking of the emotions' automatic message. The best of minds do not work well when correct data does not reach them, as in the case of the emotionally disturbed or ill, who cannot differentiate between their emotions and their minds, between what they feel and what they think.

The emotions must not be confused with conscience, which is a moral judgment about the goodness or the badness of something thought, said or done. There are no feelings directly connected with conscience. There is a tremendous tendency in good people to believe they are guilty when they feel guilty, while many evil people feel very little if any guilt. There is a great difference between guilt feelings before and after the fact of wrongdoing. The anxiety of many good people to do right, so akin to the fear of wrongdoing, is often interpreted by them as an indication of wrongdoing or guilt. Guilt feelings, so closely related to anxiety and often identified with it, come in anticipation of doing anything contrary to accepted pattern, even when the pattern was set by ignorance, or by tyrannical authority wielded unjustly or dishonestly. Innocent people often feel anxious, and/or guilty, when stopped for any reason by a policeman. Those reared in authoritarian families, or trained under authority-obedience-oriented regimes, tend to concede guilt in the face of censorious authority, to meekly accept misunderstanding, to abdicate their right to question and, sometimes, even their freedom. They do not "feel" equality in the presence of a uniform or have an awareness of their personal dignity or rights in the presence of authority. Such guilt feelings in the innocent, and the reaction to them by the good, have permitted evil to be done in the name of God and under the guise of good. Good people, faced with authority, too seldom ask the right questions or demand justice or a course of action worthy of God or of the power authority lays claim to.

True guilt feelings, like all the feelings, are very helpful and worthwhile. They are the best possible warning in the face of a situation requiring deeper thought and further consideration, before something is done hastily or irresponsibly. Acting much as the emotion of genuine anxiety does, they create sincere concern and disposition for a second good hard look before action follows. Guilt feelings after wrongdoing, of course, dispose one to regret, remorse and restitution, because they are so hard to live with. Hardened criminals have inured themselves so well to such feelings that they hardly register unless the code of thieves itself is broken. In such cases it is more fear than guilt that alerts them to what is done and the price to be paid if they are caught. The "worst" feelings do not make one bad, any more than the "best" feelings make one good. The feelings of a man never make him guilty; that comes from what he is and does, from full malice aforethought.

The emotions must not be confused with gross selfishness. Emotionally dominated people do things which are commonly misinterpreted as selfish, mainly because they cannot escape the compulsion of their feelings. That others are involved in what they do or want hardly crosses the threshhold of their consciousness. Pleasure is irresistible to them and pain is unacceptable. They are always undisciplined. The genuinely selfish person, on the other hand, is neither immature nor irresponsible. He knows what should be done and is quite capable of doing it but simply refuses to do it, chooses not to do it because it does not suit him. He lacks virtue and generally is vicious, but he is disciplined.

People who are uncomfortable when they are enjoying themselves, because of their fear of doing wrong, are also emotional cripples. God did not put an unqualified curse on pleasure nor an unqualified blessing on pain. Many "good" people find a strange comfort in pain and suffering, which they consider a mark of distinction, and even enjoy. The emotional health of such people leaves much to be desired. They are not at all like the emotionally mature people whose ability to accept unavoidable pain and suffering does keep pain within its very real limitations.

In picking out one set or category of emotions one must remember its relationship to the others, otherwise it is like discussing one key or note on the piano without reference to the instrument or to piano music. The sexual emotions cannot be isolated and understood without reference to all the emotions. But everything said about the emotions in general also applies to the sexual emotions.

Since man is by nature sexual, he must feel sexual. He is born with genitals which he must feel strongly inclined to use. There is something wrong with the person who does not feel that inclination. However there is a tremendous tendency to stress only the genital aspect of the sexual emotions. But the basic indication of normal sexual emotions is the very real need a man feels for a woman and a woman for a man, not only as a companion in copulation but as a personal companion, helpmate, confidant and lover. Male and female complement each other personally as well as sexually. When this mutual need is either suppressed or exploited, the result has to be poor intersexual relationships. People normally respond sexually to a sexual stimulus, and everyone of the opposite sex is a sexual stimulus. All other things being equal (and in practice they never are), there should be a greater interest and rapport between man and woman than between two of the same sex.

The sexual emotions can be discussed, but not understood, out of context with the sexual mores and customs of the period. People do not change but customs do. Our grandmothers would have *felt*, and been considered, quite naked in a bathing suit modest by today's standards. Modern openness has removed the taboo from the subjects of sex and sexuality so that they can be discussed now with more detachment than some other bodily functions. In actual fact, in our society, there is year-round open season for sex. There is no way that anyone can dispense himself from a personal confrontation with sex and the proper management of its related emotions. An urgent study and understanding of this matter is inescapable and vital if one is to cope with modern living. The wisdom and virtue required to manage in it come only from easy familiarity with the sexual emotions and full acceptance of one's own sexuality.

The inexperienced and undisciplined have little or no defence against their sex emotions gone wild, or the encouragement, so prevalent in our society, to exploit them. Not only is sex ridiculously considered sufficient basis for a long-term relationship, but it is widely accepted as a functional need as indispensable as eating or breathing. Many people tend to comfort themselves in these distortions of truth with a homemade conscience formed almost entirely by how they *feel*. So, too many are carried headlong into marriages they *feel* to be right because they are *in love* rather than because they love deeply and well. Lured or compelled by sex, they often eagerly burden themselves prematurely with marriage, a serious obligation they are incapable of handling, and subsequently with children they are ill equipped to raise. The children of such marriages are often conceived unwanted and gestated resentfully, and considered intruders who are denied the mature love of happy parents. They are destined to become emotional cripples, to join the protest march through life of the innumerable unloved, to make a mockery of marriage and to stand as evidence of the rarity of real love.

The sexual emotions are strong but, like all the other emotions, they are far from irresistible. They are certainly less strong than anger or fear, to say nothing of insecurity. But until they are well understood, they will continue unresisted to dominate the followers of the pied piper of sexual permissiveness. The sex-dominated person is as emotionally immature as any other emotionally dominated person, and functions beneath the level of reason, as a child, not so much immorally as emotionally.

How then do the sexual emotions work? How can emotional health be gauged from the sexual point of view?

The sex emotions do not really make themselves consciously felt until puberty. Infants do have genital awareness. Infant males do have erections and females do respond in an infantile way to sexual stimuli, but these reactions are about as purely physical as feelings can be. Such sexual awareness is on a very basic plane of consciousness. These experiences do have a very minimal emotional effect, but nothing like the effect of the emotions specifically dealt with, or avoided, on a highly conscious level. They are more physical than personal experiences, with more superficial than deep or lasting effects. They dispose, rather than compel, children towards emotional problems.

There is incontrovertible evidence of the incredible influence of the first year of life on emotional conditioning, growth and development. Infants and children require the security of a love-oriented milieu in which to experience their emotions and so gradually learn how to integrate them into real living. The emotional state of most disturbed people is correctly traced back to their childhood environment and reflects their few happy experiences, and the many unfortunate ones that inhibit their eager acceptance and promote the frightened uncertainty characterizing their emotional lives. During the childhood years there is ample opportunity to experience, and accept, the emotions in the protective atmosphere of a loving home where they can be contended with under minimal pressure. If a healthy pattern of emotional living is well begun before the severe pressure of the sexual emotions is experienced, this pattern will minimize the impact of the sexual emotions and reduce the chances of disastrous consequences of the trial and error learning process. The way the sexual emotions will be handled is determined almost completely by the way the other emotions have been met and handled prior to puberty. The emotionally healthy child moves into adolescence and adult sexual life with the assurance carried forward from prior successful emotional experience. He adjusts to sex without being dominated by his sexual feelings or fear of them. Fully accepting his sexuality, he integrates it comfortably into his loving.

The growth of children towards conscious sexuality, therefore, depends greatly on their general emotional health. Emotionally indulged children, those reared in general permissiveness, will be victims of their sex emotions, which they exploit freely for all available pleasure or suppress only to avoid possible pain. They find discipline intolerable and are in deep emotional trouble before they have any appreciable awareness of the damage being done. The problem of the overdisciplined child is as acute; prissiness, disdain for sex, snobbery and a false set of standards are not healthy signs. But the overdisciplined child, aided by the normal pull of healthy sex emotions, has a far better chance of adjusting downward to a healthy attitude than has the indulged adolescent of adjusting upward to discipline. The latter finds it nearly impossible to achieve the discipline for minimal order in his life. The course to health for the emotional slob is much more difficult than that from rigid discipline, though neither inflexibility nor flaccidity is ever a virtue.

The child of temper tantrums and sulks predictably mishandles his sexual emotions, as does the victim of unfortunate and frightening sexual childhood experience. This is likewise true of those threatened with dire moral consequences of sexual acts nearly meaningless to the child but given undue seriousness by frightened adults hypersensitive to sexual experience. Childhood discoveries, experiments and experiences must never be given a moral significance which only adult crimes could have. Young people should be adequately instructed in the normal manifestations of the sexual emotions which have nothing directly to do with morals or propriety. Certainly, the mechanical stimulation of his own newly discovered genitals by the experimenting child has none of the formal, but only the material, qualities of wrongness. Moral significance must be based on understanding and the willingness to do known evil. While masturbation often has no more moral significance for the child than a temper tantrum, because of the ignorance or secrecy usually surrounding sex the problem is not dealt with as directly or ably as are temper tantrums. When the problem is faced squarely, without preconceived notions, the stupidity of deliberate masturbation is easily established and ultimately avoided. The common occurance of masturbation does not make it desirable, much less commendable, as many counselors would have it. Even though it may be less harmful than other conditions it is still an emotional setback or failure. It reveals an exploitative tendency which is a real obstacle to the genuine outgoingness of love. It is a turning in on oneself for a pleasure not experienced outside, either through rejection, fear of rejection, or a sense of personal inadequacy. The pleasure content of masturbation is as limited as that of any feeling. Only the person who misguidedly makes any pleasure, however harmful, a good thing in itself, can recommend masturbation.

It is normal, and to be expected, that the first conscious awareness of the specifically sexual emotions, that is the venereal and very pleasurable feelings experienced in the genital areas of the body, will jolt and disturb. There is the novelty and high excitement of discovery, and an unusually intense preoccupation for a considerable time with this specific and sometimes apparently isolated function, which can be enlightening and healthy or to an equal degree morbid and unhealthy. This is a time for which sex education should prepare the child. Parents should be equipped and ready to understand it and to help to the necessary and desirable degree. However, it is to be expected that the emotionally healthy child will move into it quite naturally and should not need extraordinary help. He is alarmed and upset by apprehensive parents who project their own sexual hangups, or incompetent teachers with morbid sexual fascination. No child is ready for the sexual discovery unless he has experienced love sufficiently to sense intuitively that the human sexual act is related to loving, that it must be purposeful and tied into the over-all interests and welfare of the human person. The dignity and worthiness of human sex is part of this concept.

The purely physical aspect of sex dominates early awareness. It is far more related to self than to others. It always has moral overtones regardless of the pearls of wisdom of modern psychology or the Olympian platitudes of social philosophers to the contrary. Puberty is the expressed peak of self-awareness, intriguingly novel and somewhat overwhelming in its accompanying feelings of independence and defiance. It is the first sense of being an island in the sea of humanity, and lonely and lost in being so. There is a feeling of asocialness and of kicking off the burnt-out first-stage rocket of childhood, of being half man and half boy, of spurning yet still needing a mother. There is a vague awareness of a self-assertiveness made possible by a continuing protectiveness of home and family, the beginning of self-determination and self-sufficiency. The adolescent still retains most of the privileges without having assumed any of the more serious social obligations. He is at his freest, entering adulthood without being an adult. He is reacting sexually with a power not previously experienced. He wants to make himself, and his presence felt. Before this, long before this, he should have learned from those around him that a well-ordered emotional life is essential to successful and happy living in the relationships he has with others. If this truth has been assimilated, one has sufficient emotional health, even at this early age, for the state of loving or a realistic marriage. Youthful marriages are usually failures only because of emotional immaturity.

Sexual reactions occasion a serious and more profound attention to others. One's awareness is more acute, his desire to relate more specific, genitally directed. Here his early emotional experience manifests itself. If his experience with the outside world to which he reached eagerly and uninhibited as a child was unfortunate, he will tend to withdraw defensively, turn in on himself, become a loner. If he met indulgence and grew up uncontrolled, using his other emotions to exploit others, he will tend to exploit sexually those who attract him or awaken his sexual desires. However, if he is emotionally healthy his sexual relations will be accepted in the larger context of love; he will not misunderstand them. Whenever he reacts sexually, knowing that he relates whole person to whole person the accompanying emotions of tenderness and personal interest will not be lost on him, but will keep him love-aware as well as sex-aware. His sexual emotions will be invaluable to him as the starting point towards personal love. They will present him with the strongest impetus to relate to another person intimately, to share himself with another in a way hitherto unexperienced. He will not permit fear to choke off the accompanying emotions of tenderness, concern, generosity and self-sacrifice. The sexual emotions will stimulate him to giving and a responsibility which simply will not develop unless he understands sex correctly and integrates it into his loving. This precise experience of the sexual emotions not merely experienced but understood, more than any other is the emotional contribution to the making of a real man or woman.

At the time of the first bloom of sexual emotions, it is important to be sensitive enough to receive their message at the earliest possible moment and correctly. It is not an accident that the increased sensitivity of pubescence is noticeable by almost anyone. But unfortunately, although this high sensitivity is generally admitted, it is seldom appreciated. It is the tragedy of puberty that many do not recognize the thrust of their sexual emotions until they have reached such a pitch as to carry all before them. This can be the death of love, simply because tragic experience does not inspire one to try again to find real love. The ill-considered action, precipitated by sexual excitement, too easily deludes the young about the degree of personal relationship involved. It is virtually impossible to tell people *in love* that they do not know each other well or that their relationship is based purely on superficialities. Most people simply do not try, hoping that the structure of such relationships will crash under the weight of its own emotional content. Unfortunately the emotionally dominated acquire little wisdom and even consider their own minds antagonistic to the felt needs which dominate them. If the mind has been trained from childhood to recognize the merit of truth, its real object, and to recognize in the emotions invaluable faculties of precise, if limited competence, reporting validly only the *felt* situation, there is some hope that the limitations of the sex emotions will not only be understood but accepted. The best the emotions can reveal is the feeling *now*, present tense, about anyone. The emotions are so limited to the present that people who live by their feelings can contradict themselves from day to day, without being liars, simply because they feel differently about things when a little time has elapsed. This is nowhere truer than of the sexual emotions. They are quite incapable of expressing a personal relationship which is a matter of mind and will, past, present, and future, and the many qualities in both people which are essential to a deep loving relationship. All they can do is report a localized feeling at the moment.

Greater appreciation of the sexual emotions assures better relating to others. Every genital feeling is a sexual emotion pure and simple. It expresses infallibly nothing more or less than a need, a genital interest in, and attraction to, one of the opposite sex. However, it is at times the dominant feeling, but it should never be permitted either through ignorance or default to block out the myriad other feelings relating to a person or an object. One can develop awareness of these other feelings, which, though present, are not strong enough to make their presence felt in the sexually dominated. Each of these other feelings has a message of its own. If felt and read correctly, they make a multidimensional situation clear. They save one from domination by a single emotion and an unreal, one-dimensional pursuit—for example, the man in bed with another's wife who in the heat of passion does not even notice the husband enter the room with a gun. Other emotional stars in the sexual galaxy are tenderness, concern, protectiveness, anxiety, the joy and elation of friendly companionship and sharing, the delight of discovery of the new world of another person. These messages from the emotions, in the mature person, get just as much of a hearing as the genital ones, which may be louder but are no more meaningful. When they get that hearing, they take the rough edges and urgency away from the genital sexual emotions and present sex in the context of personal relationships and responsibility. In one who appreciates the truth, getting these messages insures the relationship against the dead end of sexploitation.

The sexual emotions can never, on their own, drive one to sexual indulgence. In this regard the sexual emotions have been given a very bad name, which they do not deserve. They dominate only when permitted, or encouraged to do so. Rather than being accepted as simple emotions, they are considered a roaring lion waiting to devour the unwary. They are endowed with a ferocity and irresistibility which no emotion naturally has. They seem to tyrannize the undisciplined and indulgent only because they fill the vacuum left in these persons by unthinkingness and weakness of will. Quite the contrary to tyrannizing, the sexual emotions make themselves felt early enough to assure their direction to a genuine relationship by anyone understanding and esteeming love for the tremendous achievement that it is. They are not toys to be played with but faculties to be employed in the interest of the whole person. Like all emotions, they call to judgment—in this instance about the place of sex in the relationship presented. They strongly suggest the management of sex rather than its domination. They make the use of sex by love possible. It is quite true that sexually dominated or fearful, sexually suppressed people, erroneously convinced that sex is bigger than the man, cannot afford the luxury of sexually stimulating situations because they will perish in them. However this is not the fault of the sexual emotions aroused in the situations but a result of the emotional ill health of the people involved, who cannot use their feelings well.

The healthy man gladly receives the information from his sexual emotions because he knows that no one need at any time be dominated by any emotion. He knows that sex is not more difficult to handle than anger, jealousy or elation. The healthy man feels adequate as a person, is convinced of his manhood and general normalcy. He can handle his emotions.

Manhood to the emotionally, sexually controlled man, is the ability to love rather than the compulsion to copulate. The sexual emotions do not frighten or panic him, nor does he engage in the silly business of deluding himself about his control by playing one emotion against another as fearful or jealous people do. His well used sexual emotions switch on his cerebral cortex which evaluates the relationship at hand and sets a course for its successful development, or, orders it aborted. Far from leading one into temptation, the sexual emotions can preserve one from it. They cannot pretend to be something they are not; they are never the basis, but merely the occasion, of love. They never manage to throw the intelligence of the mature person out of gear.

The Judeo-Christian heritage of sexual teachings and taboos, the litany of Western man's unfortunate experiences with himself and his relationships in his journey through history, caused the sexual emotions to be looked upon with a jaundiced eye. It became a virtue to suppress the sexual emotions by invoking fear, an even stronger emotion. Fear was the scapel used in the psychological surgery by which sex was removed in the delusion that chastity was possible without sex emotions. The chronic state of fear brought on sexual inadequacy; and the use of fear left people morally defenceless in situations in which they were not afraid. Much like those who avoided copulation for fear of V.D. until penicillin was discovered, or for fear of pregnancy before the Pill, there was nothing to save them from themselves when the fear of sex was removed. They then were sexually dominated as they had been fear-dominated.

Undue fear of sex drilled into young people to "protect" them from themselves not only deprives them of the occasions required for the practice of chastity, but also of the opportunity to learn to love in preparation for marriage. Nervous parents or friends, projecting their own fears, have made a virtue—erroneously called prudence, sometimes chastity—of young people's withdrawing from sexual and loving situations. Yet they can never learn to love well in any other situations. The toll of premarital unloving is obvious everywhere in the incredible number of unhappy marriages. Too many young people were encouraged to believe that love would come to them automatically through experience, or in some mysterious way other than the school of painfully acquired discipline and the power to act well in loving situations. Where sexual emotions are not experienced there is no occasion for chastity, which is the power to act lovingly under pressure of the sexual emotions. Certainly, man is not improved by replacing cultural and religious taboos with contraceptives and abortions rather than virtue and understanding. Apart from the fact that these substitutes leave him with little self-respect, they are the stuff of which emotional cripples are made—line-of-least-resistance, head-in-the-sand solutions temporizing with reality.

A common consequence of mismanagement of the sexual emotions is continual suspicion of the sexual involvement of others. Since emotionally sick people believe sex is bigger than they are, and judge others by themselves, what else could they believe about men and women associating together? They are fascinated by gossip and scandal of a sexual nature on which they feed their own suppressed and often unconscious sexual appetites. This characteristic is plainly manifest in the insatiable appetites of perfectly "nice" people for the dirty novel with little or no redeeming literary merit, reviewed and praised by commercial hacks whose acclaim gives some aura of respectability to reading it. The healthy acceptance of, and ability to love with, normal sexual feelings make sexual fantasy or furtive vicarious sex experience a superfluous bore.

The sexual arousal, so purposeful and desirable at specific and chosen times in loving marriage, need not take place in the loving of unmarried people who understand that love is much greater and broader than sex. In the loving situation they will not be carried away by their sexual emotions if they have the same understanding and control of their sexual appetites as the patient, peaceful man has of his temper. All people who, despite their inclinations to the contary, elect to do what is best have such emotional control. When man makes sex an end in itself he is claiming the genital pleasure from the mechanical function of the sex organs as high human achievement, which it is not . If it were, one could not question the emotional health or stability of people in seemingly stable marriages who suddenly find themselves in love with a stranger and desert their husbands or wives and children, for whom they feel little love. These people do not understand what the human achievement of love is or the virtue and discipline which strengthen it.

CHAPTER SIX

Understanding Sex

To understand sex is to have a realistic awareness of the place of the genital function in the development and maturity of both the human person and the race. This includes not merely the mechanical functions of the genitals but the meaning of the male-female relationship in its personal and social ramifications. The genital function alone equally involves the tsetse fly, the the giant panda, the ape, and man: but human sex involves the whole meaning and purpose of man, who shares nothing essentially human with the animal world. What man is and does today, through sex, profoundly influences future generations. The heavy burden on man to make wise and right decisions of greater significance than personal pleasure or advantage requires his understanding of sex. Only deep respect for human sex can save genetics from the caprice of scientists.

The process of understanding anything has several steps. Man gets the picture through his senses (apprehends); the picture is filtered through the emotions (the impact of experience) to the mind, which understands (comprehends); accumulated understanding facilitates practical judgments through which wisdom is acquired. The end product of understanding sex is the wisdom and virtue to live well with it, to integrate it into one's loving. For the emotionally healthy person this is no problem, but for the emotionally ill, that is, the emotionally dominated or withdrawn, it is very difficult to live with sex. Battered by their clamouring emotions, they do not get the picture in the first place, or if they do, it is badly distorted. They lack almost all objectivity because they see and hear only what they like to see and hear. They are emotionally incapable of processing experience correctly; practical judgment is beyond them, and they acquire neither understanding nor wisdom. They either wallow in sex, to which they are irresistibly addicted, or withdraw in the face of it to avoid hurtful experience. Sensing that they are made to love, they have not a clue as to how to go about it, nor any hope of achieving it; loneliness is inevitably ahead of them.

Understanding sex means much more than the knowledge and experience to achieve orgasm. Like the automobile, sex is much easier to use than to understand. Being sexually equipped carries no more right to function sexually than buying an automobile carries the right to drive. Yet most people "feel" they have the right to the pleasures and privileges of sex without the sobering responsibility to use it well. Understanding sex provides man with the knowledge required to use his over-all welfare (and that of others, which he equates with his own) rather than his "feelings" to measure the acceptability of both the pain and pleasure of sex. The mind and the will can completely control the sexual faculties, from the genitals themselves to the most urgent sexual emotions. Sex is understood when its real place in the life of man is established, and is efficaciously understood when the person actually lives that way. The man who loves accepts all the restraints on any of his sexual inclinations that are detrimental to interpersonal relationships. Understanding sex makes this possible.

The protest against those puritanical, erroneous notions of sex which retard man's growth and development as a sexual person, is legitimate. The rebellion against not only prissiness but any restraint, however, now threatens to keep man less than his genitals, since fear of sex is being replaced by sex itself as a dominant force in human living. It is no improvement to replace one form of tyranny with another. Genital sex will dominate man unless it is incorporated into loving, which is what understanding sex is all about. Happiness in sex does come from its use in a permanent, exclusive, loving relationship between man and woman. That is the one basis on which sex works really well. The problems that irresponsible and unloving sex creates in broken homes, unwanted, emotionally crippled children and the current abortion industry are but a part of the high cost of misunderstood, misused sex.

The human sexual drive, unlike that in animals, is meant to accomplish the preservation of the species with love and the freedom vital to love. Everything great and wonderful about a human being should go into his sexual life. To disdain sex is to be contemptuous of man's integrity, to misunderstand the meaning of the word human. Man's happiness requires that he live happily with sex, neither suppressing nor exploiting it. He does share sex with the animals but his sex is as human as his intelligence.

The human sexual dimension enables men and women to relate to each other in a most basic way, and when sex is not understood even this simplest of interpersonal relationships is unattainable. Sex understood, however, makes it plain that the purely sexual relationship is the simplest and easiest, and therefore the least rewarding and fulfilling, of all human relationships. Those whose best performance is in the purely sexual embrace have a very limited scope indeed. Social man, however sexually active he may be, is inevitably driven into the isolation of loneliness (living suicide) when he is incapable of a loving relationship. This is very obvious in our affluent and liberal society where sex is so universally and easily available, and yet has done nothing to reduce the incredible toll of loneliness, but in fact, adds to it.

That sex education should be mandatory in these times is crystal clear. Education prepares one for life. Who doubts the importance of sex in modern life? It is plain that the functions and manifestations of sex are so confused with amorous or conjugal love that only genuine love can save most people from destruction on the jagged edges of sexual living. If sex is important, then love is much more important. There is just no way that one will understand human loving without understanding the far simpler matter of sex. Understanding sex makes it plain that the absence of genital sex is far less consequential than the absence of love. Ignorance of sex makes marriage an empty promise of paradise and chastity a cruel, unnatural hoax, while understanding sex opens the way in marriage to deep loving rapport in the most personal relationship, and makes it possible to discover in chastity a reasonable and fulfilling way to love. Understanding sex prevents its gross exaggeration in married love, as it prevents sex from dominating the loving relationships so vital to the single person. It prevents sex from choking married love to death, and assures that in unmarried loving nothing essentially human is missing.

The easy decision that sex education is essential does nothing to make it possible, let alone effective. Sex plays such a role in the evolution of man and his responsible behaviour that it is far better ignored than taught badly. It seems a simple thing to have parents instruct their children in what are simplistically called "the facts of life", and few question that it is primarily their job to do so. However, even when the "facts" can be agreed upon, few parents have the understanding, the teaching know-how, or even the basic terminology of sex required for the job. Teaching sex involves much more than anatomy, physiology and biology. It involves the psychological, emotional and spiritual dimensions of man as well. The present backlash against sex education comes from the disastrous social and psychological consequences of sexual permissiveness attributed rightly and wrongly to inadequate sex education. It is a catastrophe to accept the pleasure potential of sex outside the context of society's welfare. The allusion to sex as "the facts of life" typifies the wrong approach to understanding it. There are obvious, easily verifiable facts of sex, like its anatomy and physiology, which are easily taught and learned. But there are many facets of sex and sexuality so inseparable from a sound philosophy of the purpose of man and his social life that sex education makes no sense without them. The knowledge of sexual anatomy and physiology must be directed to the complete role of sex in human life, and to the basic purpose of human life itself. Sex education must be approached also with the objectivity sought in language and science studies. Man can welcome the truth as much in his personal sexual life, if he is so disposed, as in other phases of his life. In the truth man finds his way to love as the basis of his sexual activity, when he has the goodwill to do so. Through goodwill—love—sex is fully humanized and plays its role in man's personal life and for the welfare of the race. It is the purpose of sex education to see that it does.

The power to put sex information to the best use requires more than education. And basic to human life is the realization that knowledge of facts carries no guarantee that they will be well used. Thus it is totally unrealistic to think that one who knows better will necessarily do better, since what one does depends on one's convictions and one's moral character, or virtue. Understanding sex will establish the role of sex in life but living that role requires personal principle. Many with knowledge of sex have little ability, desire or intention to use it for anything but their own enjoyment, which takes it completely out of the context of real life. But sex *has* to be lived well; sex really matters in public as well as private life, to a much greater degree than almost any academic subject. Thus sex education by hedonists, who through arrogance or ignorance dismiss the moral aspects of sex, has to be unacceptable. Their contempt for restraints other than those acceptable to themselves disqualifies them as sex educators. Those who too glibly pass on their own limited and badly thought-out ideas, their peculiar hang-ups and behaviour patterns, violate their trust as teachers. Sex made a matter of pure academics is taken out of life's context and the way is opened to exploitative pleasure addiction. Plainly, sex education requires teachers of extraordinary insight, intelligence, understanding and moral goodness. It is obviously a formidable undertaking.

Most parents trust only those sex educators having a deep understanding of the whole subject in all its ramifications, for whom sex is a matter of personal convictions as well as social concern. This involves an apppreciation of moral values originating in the history of sex and contributing to the wisdom to avoid the devastating misuse of sex. The prophets of the new sexual freedom, ignoring essential moral values, actually preach a new kind of slavery. While invoking cultural and religious superstition to justify throwing off every restrictive obligation, they provide no answers to the problems of pleasure addiction, sexual licence, and the incredible devastation of unloving. The deadly results of incomplete sex instruction are most obvious only when the headlong course to personal destruction is all but irreversible.

Another problem in sex education is the narrow, proud person who tolerates mistakes in general learning but is strangely intolerant of even honest mistakes in learning sex. Sex education carries no special dispensation from error even for those who wish it did. Sexual mistakes, far from being catastrophic or irremediable, often supply in humility what is lost in chastity; they do carry with them the learning value which St Augustine so thoroughly appreciated, often occasioning a healthy compensatory honesty. While no formal sex education can take the place of good example, parents, teachers, counselors and friends contribute immensely to emotional maturity and personal growth by helping others to recognize, accept and learn by their mistakes. Sex education can never be the exclusive responsibility of any one institution or person.

Proper sex education should prepare the way for the inevitable sexual experience of the developing child. It can be categorically stated that the reaction of the child to sexual experience is the same as his reaction to any other normal experience, except where, through ignorance or prejudice, he has been conditioned to apprehension or fear of sex, or led prematurely by seduction into sexual indulgence. The child can be disposed to sexual pleasure addiction by his acquired emotional reactions to pain and pleasure. Indulgence in pleasure rewards by misguided parents is just as prejudicial to learning through sexual experience as is punishing a frightened child surprised in some sexual discovery. The child not already addicted to pleasure seldom finds the pleasure of sex irresistable.

Ideally the child should learn as quickly and as well as possible to accept fully the fact of sex, to understand its urgency and compulsion at the feeling level, without being deluded that it is beyond control, or that control is unnecessary. Pyschiatrists, psychologists and counselors who dismiss masturbation as unimportant, as having little or no symptomatic significance, deprive children of the understanding needed for the sexual control indispensable to emotionally healthy living. Healthy acceptance of sexual experience is vital in acquiring the power to direct all lesser functions to the good of the whole person and of society. While the child discovered at masturbation should not be threatened, neither should he be awarded a medal. He should be intelligently guided to interests outside himself which absorb the attention otherwise wasted on self-pity and self-indulgence. Children who are starved for affection, who have experienced rejection, real or imagined, are severely handicapped in the initial discovery of genital pleasure. They are often, or even generally, inclined to turn into themselves, in masturbation, as a compensatory pleasure mechanism, with varying but always undesirable results.

Masturbation is begun for any number of reasons, from quite innocent, accidental discovery of easily available and ever accessible pleasure, to the prankish, seductive explorations encouraged by peers or older companions. Subsequent studies seem to support Kinsey's figures for masturbation—that is, that 90% of boys and

50% of girls masturbate any number of times from once to habitually. Those who masturbate only once, or rarely, can in no way be considered *bona fide* masturbators. They certainly do not bear the emotional scars of sexual pleasure addiction. They have no delusions about the urgency or inevitability of sexual misuse. Kinsey's figures do indicate, however, the extent of the undiscriminating search of children for pleasure rewards (much wants more), which they must learn to accept when beneficial, and to deny themselves when prejudicial. It is utterly ridiculous to accept masturbation, however statistically normal, as a healthy, harmless outlet for emotional tensions. Like a temper tantrum, masturbation is one way of releasing emotional pressure but it does not replace emotional control. Only the mistake of equating emotional control with emotional repression makes masturbation seem preferable to worse things. At best, it is always only the lesser of evils. It is usually an early symptom of predisposition to addiction. The emotional health of the child requires willingness to accept his failures; and masturbation, like a temper tantrum, is a failure. No failure is commendable, however understandable and acceptable as a fact. Despite statistics, masturbation, like the measles, is not made good because of the number experiencing it. Statistical games contribute nothing to the development of children into emotionally healthy adults.

A crucial stage in understanding sex is reached in the sexual experience of puberty, the physiological plea of sex for recognition and acceptance. As sexual maturity begins in the emotionally unrepressed person, pleasurable sexual feelings increase their pressure in the livelier flow and ebb of blood through the muscles and nerves of the sexual sensory centres. This experiential awareness of the sex pleasure factor is essential to maturity. At this time sexual needs are felt with a highly exciting and compelling novelty. Curiosity, the stimulus to understanding, is unusually high. The growing boy experiences full erections both in his sleep and while awake, resulting from internal and external physical and psychological stimuli. Those who deplore or dread this "thrust from innocence to experience" would delay maturity and deprive the boy of the very experience vital to understanding and coping with sex. To cope with sex means to develop the necessary control to live successfully with it.

Unprovoked nocturnal seminal emissions, as pleasurable as, and usually involving, orgasm, take place with some regularity in the boy, with a force which alerts him to his manhood and its responsibilities. Inherent in the experience of the erection is the dawning comprehension of the sexual purpose for his penis, and a strong new awareness of the desire to so use it. He may or may not masturbate or have intercourse, but even where moral principles and self-discipline are sufficient for continence, it is important that through the experience of the erection and emission, the place of sex in his life is gradually understood and fully accepted. He gradually comprehends sex as the combined operation of two free, responsible people bringing to the act not only their functional equipment but enough mutual love and respect to establish a lasting relationship. This relationship provides the secure atmosphere into which children ought to be born.

The same basic process takes place in the girl, though not necessarily with the same conscious awareness. The Western cultural penalty on the "good" woman for discussing sex openly only partially explains her lag in conscious awareness, knowledge and acceptance of sex. She should be helped to understand what her body is trying to make plain, that she wants the love of a man, a home, and his child. She too becomes acutely aware of the flow and ebb of sexual sensation in her body and should know the precise meaning of these sensations. The increased flow of blood to her clitoris and other genital organs makes her aware of sexual pleasure and her basic need for sexual fulfilment. She also experiences the pressing sexual needs normal to her menstrual cycle. She senses a vaginal emptiness, and an expectant, eager readiness for intercourse, a physical, psychological and personal anxiety to be filled. As with her brothers, it is most important for her, too, to use these experiences to gradually understand and accept the place of sex in her life, and its relationship to loving. Each sex should be made aware of the parallel experience of the opposite sex, which seems so different but which in reality is so much the same. These sexual experiences are essentially the bases of understanding sex.

The normal man is attracted to women, and considers, however fleetingly, having intercourse with every woman to whom he is attracted. He falls easily in love with one, and probably several women, both before and after his commitment to marriage. If he is mature, thoughtful and disciplined he will be deeply in love with the one he marries. He should, however, freely consider having intercourse with other women, that is to say, insist that his mind follow, constructively and responsibly, the train of thought suggested by his feelings. It is when he looks at the sex act in the context of the relationship, rather than in isolated fantasy, that the occasion for the virtue of fidelity is presented, that he is challenged to place the emphasis on the person rather than the body. By nature man wants the intercourse for which he is born and equipped; his normal inclination is to have intercourse often and with many women. It is when he thinks the matter through (which requires little time, and should not be confused with daydreaming, or wallowing in visions of a thousand and one nights of sexual delights) and imagines that he has had intercourse with the one attracting him, that he then asks himself how such an act can be reconciled with true love, his present obligations, and the real good of the persons involved. Honest answers easily disabuse him of delusions, expose philandering for what it is and make plain the impossible complications it introduces into real life. Only the dreamer or escapist can see advantages in contradictions to true love, in taking sex out of the context of reality, the loving relationship. It is easy to have intercourse, but to be meaningful it must be had with one to whom one relates deeply and personally. Promiscuity makes a shambles of one's personal relations and one's happiness. Sexual experience makes this plain; it also makes plain how meaningful intercourse is in the living security of the lasting commitment.

Fundamental to understanding sex is the conviction that man is greater than sex—its master, not its slave. Those exploiting others for personal pleasure twist themselves beyond recognition as human. Morally, they should be pariahs; but our society is a sick one which ostracizes only the visibly ugly, in which it is much less acceptable to smell bad than to be bad. Any reasonable man accepts restraints on his temper; restraints on his sexual life are even more reasonable. The social aspect of sexual life is inescapable and therefore never anyone's private business. Society is the beneficiary of sexual life; it is the milieu of sexual existence. Sex has no meaning when restricted to the individual, therefore it can never be a matter of personal whim. Sex is always disordered unless the whole man grows through it. It must likewise increase the stature of his partner and of society. Other individuals, and society, suffer from the sex-dominated man or woman. The part that exploitative sex plays in crime and the rackets is obvious. The taxable income from crime would provide half the required operating expense of modern government. But the real tax paid on commercial sex, perversion, and addictive pleasure is the reduced stature of man himself.

Neither is sex merely for breeding. A great disservice is rendered sex when the physical production of children is made a virtue in itself. A subfunction of man's dominant powers to think and to love, sex is degraded when used in a thoughtless or unloving way. It is not a matter merely of instinct, physiological or biological drive, or emotional compulsion—not an end in itself, justified by the thrills it provides. It is a highly human act which, when done lovingly, may produce loved and loving children. The sexual controls built into man are enough to assure it being so used by anyone wanting to so use it. To do so man merely needs the motivation, the convictions of a loving person.

The built-in sexual controls are well illustrated by the physiology of blushing. (It has been wisely stated that man is the only creature who blushes, and the only one with reason to.) Blushing indicates emotional insecurity, undue shame or embarrassment. One simply cannot blush if he is relaxed; one need not blush if he is controlled. A blush is the retention of blood in the head as the heart pumps faster and the return flow to the heart is restricted by tension. Pressure forces the dammed-up blood to the facial tissues. On relaxation the dam opens, normal circulation returns and the blushing ceases. A similar tension is equally required for the erection of the penis or the clitoris. When sex is understood there is very early awareness of sexual excitement; the mind moves into action and the will takes control, if desired, well before full sexual arousal occurs. When one is motivated by a greater good (or desire) the simple command to relax causes the sexual arousal to quickly subside. The same physical effect can be experienced when the attention is diverted to something more pressing or urgent, including what is demanded by the best interests of the stimulated or stimulator. Sexual arousal is interrupted by any more dominant stimulus, such as the external threat of force or some urgent contingency. Anyone who has as much motivation to reduce sexual arousal as he has to control blushing, stuttering or any other emotional manifestation based on the tension of excitment, has adequate controls at his disposal to love well without getting bogged down in sex.

Those who deny this control are either incredibly self-indulgent, or are unaware of man's ability to master any voluntary situation in which he finds himself, or simply have no desire to use self-control. The person who can accept pleasure without being carried away by it readily accepts the built-in mechanisms of sexual control. For him, it is self-evident that sexual fulfillment consists not in using sex as one wishes, pleases or feels, but in achieving a happy life. Pleasure itself is purely experiential not a moral matter; its use is a matter of wisdom and judgment. The best management of pleasure and pain is the only reason for everyman's innate power of self-control. Every function of man is essentially controllable by him. Certainly when a stronger emotion so easily inhibits a weaker one, the will obviously can control them all. Thus love and hate provide the strongest motivations of man and both can certainly dominate the genital function even in the most erotic situations.

It is easy to find numerous other examples of sexual inhibition, or control. Sickness or hormone imbalance can cause temporary impotence. The inhibiting factors in psychological impotence, or frigidity, are plainly obvious. Any dominating emotion—fear, anger, resentment, or even indifference—inhibits the sexual emotions, for the simple reason that the inhibiting power is there. Similar specific control mechanisms in the body are the basis for the fantastic control exotic dancers exercise over individual muscles. Some very recent experiments on the autonomic nervous systems of rats have demonstrated their ability to control, for food reward, not only their own heart rate and blood pressure but even the vasodilation of the blood vessels of their right or left ears! Man certainly has these controls at his disposal too; he needs only the motivation and discipline to use them. He will hopefully be inspired to do so when he understands sex sufficiently to accept that it is tied primarily into his personal life of happiness, and then into his emotional life of pleasure.

The compelling force of sex is generally accepted as all but irresistible because it generally is not resisted. Either sufficient motive, or the required self-discipline, or the understanding of the control mechanisms is lacking. The actual compulsion to sex is attributed to sex itself instead of to the contagious nature of sexual excitement. But laughter and tears are as contagious and compelling as sexual excitement, to say nothing of nausea. Few can resist nausea in the presence of a violently vomiting person, yet it is quite controllable. The stimulus can be killed by changing one's focus from it. Intense interest in the sick person cuts right across the stimulus of nausea, as does joy in being of help, or the satisfaction of helping in the rejection of the sickening substance. Doctors, nurses and other attendants of the sick become so conditioned to resist nausea that they are all but immune to its stimulus. A disciplined, strong-willed person can remain relaxed and calm, and so place himself beyond the stimulus of sexual excitement. Naturally, the greatest incentive to do that is the true and deep love of a person whose real good excludes the sexual function temporarily or even permanently. However, to control sexual excitement one must be a strong person, and if not a virtuous, at least a very proud person. But the potential control is there, given the motive, the goodwill, and the understanding of the control processes related to the sexual function.

The incredibly sensitive nerves of the sexual organs do respond beautifully to physical and psychological stimuli, but neither necessarily nor automatically. All nerve control centres including the sexual ones are governed by the cerebral cortex, the computer programmed by the mind. Yet most people doubt the possibility of handling sexual excitement maturely and responsibly because they believe they must be carried irresistibly to genital climax regardless of its wisdom, emptiness, wrongness, or even criminality. Although sexual domination is prejudicial and personally destructive, and ultimately leads to unhappiness, few accept that sexual control is possible, let alone desirable or necessary.

If sexual arousal or stimulation were automatic, how could the psychologically impotent man or frigid woman be explained? How explain the man who performs well privately but simply cannot do so publicly? The control of the male gynaecologist examining patients? The unacceptability of sexual overtures is generally enough to inhibit sex arousal. The most sensual person can be temporarily impotent because greater emotional pressure focuses his attention elsewhere. Few people could respond sexually in a busy shopping plaza, however excited they might become about the same person in other circumstances. The nerve sensations from the sexual organs can be ignored whenever there is sufficient reason for doing so, as any husband who has vainly tried to stimulate an indifferent wife has learned. The loving person has the best motives in the world for exercising his sexual inhibiting powers; the indulgent, promiscuous, selfish person has little or none. This tremendous power of emotional control is rediscovered and developed by every alcoholic, chain smoker, compulsive eater or habitual masturbator who faces the truth and does what he knows is best, regardless of his feelings.

Sexual inhibition for inhibition's sake is ridiculous, but who would accuse a loving mother of being ridiculous when she terminates sexual intercourse to go quickly to an injured child? Who would criticize the loving spouse from refraining from intercourse when his mate is ill or injured? In similar vein, the celibate is not abusing his sexual inhibiting power when he invokes it, to an extent which precludes marriage and a family of his own, to serve others lovingly for life.

However compelling or pleasurable sexual intercourse may be, man has the potential intelligence, goodwill and physical controls to choose to function sexually or not, according to whether it is in his own best interests, those of others, or those of society itself. Many people, in the face of an attractive invitation to sexual intercourse, decline because of fidelity to their partners, the unwisdom of involvement, fear of subsequent betrayal or of getting caught. The fact that chastity seems unusual in our society does not discount the power to be chaste, but merely indicates the lack of sufficient understanding, motivation, discipline and love.

The person who recognizes, accepts and learns to live with his sexual emotions will understand sex fairly well. The male must feel like a male, and the female like a female. Such feelings make living as a fully human being the challenge that it is. To reject this challenge and accept one's sexual function on a purely pleasure level is to function subhumanly. Understanding sex demands the mature acceptance of the inherent sexual attraction always present in the development of intersexual relationships. This acceptance then requires the self-discipline to direct the sexual life lovingly.

All sexual stimuli can be neutralized, or dominated, by stronger stimuli to contrary emotions. The ferocious knock of the jealous husband on the door of the hideaway lovenest certainly creates very sexually inhibiting emotions. However, to promote other strong emotions, such as fear, to control sexual desires is disastrous, since such action assures immaturity and instability. Misuse of the emotions can never replace the real virtue and character through which loving people use sexually inhibiting mechanisms properly for the right reasons. The puritanical atmosphere of the strict home, and the moral family environment of a small town, because they more often developed fear than virtue, were poor preparations for urban living with its swinging society and permissive anonymity.

Sex can never be understood by those attributing moral qualities to the sexual emotions. Many "good" people consider sexual feelings occasions of sin, or temptations. They are seen as a threat to virtue rather than as awakening one to the beginning of a relationship. These people have been generally brainwashed into believing that sex is bigger than man, and they either accept the inevitability of being carried away by the most normal sexual feelings, or they freeze in the face of them and allow themselves to be driven from a loving situation by their feelings. People of high moral awareness often tend to morbid fear of the genuine tenderness which elicits sexual feelings akin to those experienced in erotic situations. The minor genital discharge experienced through loving tenderness puts them into severe anxiety, even panic. Yet it is as normal as the tear shed in joy or sorrow; it need have no erotic significance whatever. When such a mechanical reaction is dismissed for what it is, having no more significance than a blush, the sex feelings remain minimal, and anxiety vanishes. Panic does nothing to help one distinguish fear from guilt or anxiety, but easily magnifies feelings into motives, blows mechanical responses into deliberate acts, converts pleasure into sin, thus making understanding of sex impossible. Anxiety creates tension which exaggerates any emotional response, including the sexual, and makes the physical effects more difficult to cope with and the psychological aftermath often devastating. Such reactions, often create the fear, in perfectly good people, that they are potentially at least, satyrs or nymphomaniacs.

Normal sexual emotions are the occasion of the practice of chastity. The person with suppressed sexual emotions thus does not acquire the virtue of chastity against the time when it is needed. On the other hand, when anxiety, guilt, fear and shame accompany the most normal sexual feelings, the power of sex has to seem overwhelming, and the practice of chastity impossible. Sexual feelings are normally present in all interpersonal relationships and are the very stuff of chastity. The sexual emotions quickly reveal to the mature, virtuous person the nature of the situation he is in, and he refuses to be frightened from the challenge to love by the small degree of sexual agitation he feels. All sexual situations present the risk of tragic mistakes, but no greater mistake can be made than letting the sexual emotions drive one from the loving situation which requires the virtue of chastity to assure its development.

The emotions provide the pieces of the jigsaw puzzle of life, and with the help of the imagination the mind programs them through the computer of the brain. It takes considerable imagination to understand the place of the emotions in life, to so program pain and pleasure into real life that the former is not rejected when beneficial and the latter not indulged in when harmful. There is a general tendency to shortcircuit the imagination's vital role in understanding, a role which is especially important in understanding sex. When through ignorance of its function it is wasted, the imagination is easily made the scapegoat for all kinds of abuses.

A function of the mind, the imagination is not the mind, nor the emotions, nor fantasy, which is its work. It is the faculty of ingenuity, inventiveness. Vision gestates in the womb of the imagination to deliver progress. It produced the tools with which man built, and arranged the sounds with which he communicated and the numbers with which he counted, measured and weighed. Every useful invention of man is evidence of the imagination well used. It is the faculty of projection and planning. To understand sex, the mind must get the picture. The imagination is the picture tube pulling the intellectual and sensitive memories together, relating the experiences required for ingenious thinking. Genital sex requires little if any imagination. It functions automatically, unless inhibited, in response to physical or psychological stimuli. Imagination negotiates genital sex to love. It provides the blueprints for authentic loving situations in which man learns to give despite every inclination to get. The imagination previews the emotional stimuli experienced in related fields and makes it possible to anticipate and manage any normal venture into loving.

Before imagination can program sex into the loving process, it must liberate one from the ridculous domination of sex which makes man, momentarily at least, less than his genitals. The imagination does have the power to seduce, to present graphically orgies of unlimited delight, but only when it is abused rather than used. It is the unimaginative who can be enticed by the strip tease. A little imagination reveals what the tease addict hopes to see and explodes the false promise. The imagination lays out quite clearly all that sex has to offer and finds it wanting, for sex is not all people want. Those who understand sex are not deceived by its limited dividends. The imagination can take one through the mirage of sexual pleasure to the very real happiness of love. The most imaginative use of sex is not by the people who indulge sexually but by those who use sex commercially to exploit the unimaginative. Imaginative people quickly realize the phony and are seldom deluded by a one-dimensional situation. Wise people do not fall for something as easily explored and quickly exhausted as sex, but placing sex into the context of real life they move ahead imaginatively to achieve loving relationships, visualizing the true needs of others and the means of fulfilling them. The imagination provides the plans through which love is fruitful and rewarding.

The imagination, like sex, is meant to be the servant, rather than the master, of the man. However, it must be made to serve rather than let run riot, as it does in the lives of the undisciplined. One bogged down in sexual fantasies is sick. Imagination gone wild can so isolate sex from real life that it appears great in itself. Sexual pleasure can seem like an adequate reward for the intolerable situations it leads to or the heartbreaks inseparable from it outside the context of love. The fear of using the imagination badly, born of sad experience, unfortunately leads many to believe that it cannot be used well.

The mind uses the imagination to produce the master plan for understanding sex and from that plan lays out the man-hours of constructive work required for handling sex properly, integrating it into love and life. Applied to personal relationships, a well used imagination clearly portrays, in time for correction, the disaster of sexual compulsion, the chaos of unresisted sexual desire. It presents with compelling clarity the comparison of the fleeting pleasure of orgasm with the enduring happiness and security of love. It makes it clear that the genitals, like the imagination itself, cannot fulfill their function when used like a toy, for one's own amusement. Only those people who misuse the imagination to build their own dream worlds of escape could delude themselves that sex can be equated either with personal relationships or with happiness. The divorce courts are clogged with marriages, based on sexual attraction, which a little imagination would have exposed as hopeless from the beginning.

The runaway imagination, like the loan shark, insists that you can play now and pay later; the directed imagination tells you just how much you will pay later. The imagination, which created the myth of sex appeal for commerical purposes, can also explode it, debunk promises which cannot be kept, expose relationships which are dead ends. It also reveals the cultural hang ups and ignorance which portray women as being more interested in love and less interested in sex, deeper, more faithful, virtuous and religious than men. The properly operating imagination shows men and women as made for each other, much more alike as human beings than different. They are necessarily alike because they are complementary. The imagination sees it as the way of woman to open up personally, much more than sexually, to the personal penetration of the man she loves. And this is counterparted by the equal eagerness of the man to open up to the personal penetration of the woman's love which envelops him. The knowledgeable woman (and no one is knowledgeable without an efficacious imagination) is very aware that no sexual opening is nearly as important as her personal opening in love. Her qualities as a person, friend and companion are far more valued by her than those of her body. She does not depend on externals, deceit, beauty aids or psychological cover-ups which betray her insecurity. It is plain to her that an attractive person's body is *always* attractive, for beauty is a personal rather than a physical thing.

The woman understanding sex appreciates the vulnerability of her body to the thrust of a man. She knows that her real protection is his love of her, his trust in her. But she also appreciates the man's vulnerability to her psychological thrust. He too knows that the only protection he has from hurt is the love of the woman for him. Men and women are equally vulnerable and interdependent; both are capable of deep hurt from misplaced trust. The directed imagination presents this cold reality to both lover and loved, warning them against the disaster of premature sexual involvement.

Sex appeal in no way assures enduring relationships, and in fact deflects the genuine interest of the best and most discerning people. Experience sadly reveals how seldom a real person lives behind the facade of physical beauty. Physically attractive people, often unable to inspire or maintain personal relationships, need promiscuity to keep sex from becoming a complete bore. Boredom is impossible in love and friendship because of the continuing discovery of new dimensions of personality. The imaginative find the exploration of another person far more exciting, challenging and rewarding than the exploration of a body. A body can share sex but it takes a person to share love.

Understanding sex makes it plain how love is short-circuited by overeagerness to copulate. The apostles of sex are emotional children, forever eating the icing off the cake. Those who do not understand sex mine it for every last sliver of pleasure while love goes down the drain. However interesting, sex is a brief experience; love is a lasting experience with an interesting person. The directed imagination fastens the precise limits of sexual pleasure and relates sex correctly to the loving life.

The study of sex, undertaken by thoughtful, able people of integrity, will clear the way to the study of the power to love. More than anything else, unreasonable delay led those unwilling to be dominated by sex to choose, unhappily, not to love at all. The mature man, through love, enters a sexual union with a woman whom he chooses because of her lovable qualities. Their relationship neither begins nor ends with the sexual one but endures and matures in a personal relationship with common interests. eagerness to share in a lasting personal commitment. To understand and use sex properly man must see that he can, and decide that he will, love. Unfortunately, man's intelligence is much better developed than his good will. To operate for something more than his immediate personal pleasure demands an accepted set of standards, and virtue—the power to do what ought to be done. Without these love will remain the secret of a very few.

To understand sex means to function better not only sexually but personally. Man functions best when genuinely loving, which he cannot be without understanding sex. Ignorance of sex is not merely a tremendous obstacle to loving, but even to relating to other people, which is the beginning of love. When that obstacle has been removed the way to love is open. When science accepts the real relationship of man's genitals to his power of love, behavioural scientists will refuse to discuss human sex apart from love.

CHAPTER SEVEN

The Power to Love

Nowhere is the image of God in man so evident as in the deep, loving interpersonal relationship in which one human being looks at another and loves him. Man is never happier or more fulfilled, more virtuous and less vicious than when he loves. He is never more of a man, or a better person, than when he is keenly aware of, and most willing to fulfil, the true needs of his fellow man. This is love. God is truly manifest in the man who loves endlessly, simply because he can see God in all, any man, every man. Such love soon uncovers the image of God in one's unlovable neighbour and then works its miracle of changing unloving man to loving man.

Loving is the source of all man's happiness, as distinct from his pleasure. Only loving man is a genuine man of peace. He alone has security enough to see and confront his prejudices. Love is the broad base of all interested personal relationships. It is man's happiness to look out and away from himself, to see all that is beautiful and good, and to feel the privilege of living in the midst of it all, contributing to it, giving out from his depths, sharing, loving. Through the power of love man empties himself of the sadness of failure and fills himself with the joy that is out there, sensing that it is all big and wonderful and made for him, wanting desperately to be a real part of it all.

The power to love underlies man's prayer life, his ability to relate to God, the maker of all things, with a deep sense of gratitude for being. Who cannot thank God for that cannot love, because he cannot get his attention off himself, either to God or to man. He is too sick to see the other person.

To doubt the value or count the cost of loving is to deny God. The belief that Christ is God in flesh, the expressed Love of God,

God's Word made flesh, is supported by His teaching. His message was quite worthy of God, that man should love, would find his fulfilment in loving. Jesus said: "You must love the Lord your God with all your heart, with all your soul, and with all your mind. This is the greatest and the first commandment. The second resembles it: you must love your neighbour as yourself. On these two commandments hang the whole Law and the Prophets also." (Matthew 22:37-40).

Great men have shown by devoting their whole lives, even dying for their neighbour, that such love is certainly possible, fulfilling and rewarding. The problem of loving is always the cost. Wealth, intelligence, energy and time build a better material world, but self is the cost of a loving world, giving not one's substance but oneself. Man must be willing to lose himself to find himself, was the way Christ put it. Money cannot eliminate poverty, hunger or discrimination; dedicated, loving people can. People who want to be somebody without spending themselves are shocked when St. Paul tells them plainly that unloving people are nothing, nobodies. Life without loving is nothing.

Christ was very clear about how man should pass through the emotional bogs of self-indulgence which keep him subhuman, unloving. He said: "You have learned how it was said: You must love your neighbour and hate your enemy. But I say this to you: love your enemies and pray for those who persecute you; in this way will you be sons of your Father in heaven ... For if you love those who love you what right have you to claim any credit? Even the tax-collectors do as much do they not?" (Matthew 5:43-47) Was Christ asking the impossible? As a a matter of fact, the person who will not love his enemies will never love his friends. Both loves require the same quality, virtue—that is, the power to do what ought to be done regardless of one's feelings.

Love, as used in this book, is the power to see and the willingness to fulfil the true needs of another. This definition removes the apparent contradiction of loving one's enemies. Love is the power to do what is good for the other person, friend or enemy. After all one feels as strongly inclined to exploit one's friends as to destroy one's enemies. Both feelings give one equal pleasure, the same kind of delight. Love, on the contrary, consists in doing right by all. The young man feels the desire to copulate with the young lady he claims to love, as strongly as he feels the desire to crush his enemies. The love that makes it plain to him that he cannot take advantage of one he loves makes it equally plain that he cannot take advantage of an enemy.

Love demands the objectivity to equate the needs of anyone, acquaintance or stranger, friend or foe, with one's own. It demands the discipline to treat even strangers and enemies as human beings, with the dignity and respect due them as fellow men, brothers and sisters. It demands the wisdom to differentiate between real needs and wishes or emotional desires. Love distinguishes between fulfilment and enjoyment by giving rightness and goodness priority over pleasure and pain. Actually the key word in loving is *goodwill*. The loving man has always the ability to will the good of the other person; he is prepared to pay the real cost of peace, however great.

Peace was promised by the angels at the birth of Christ to men of *goodwill*, that is, to loving men. Peace on any other terms is a contradiction, a mere truce in the fighting for the convenience of both parties. Imposed peace is conquest. There can be peace in the world only when treaties are negotiated by people on each side intent on achieving the best interests of the other side, which they rightly and wisely identify with their own. The armed standoff, as the whole world knows only too well, is very expensive and always temporary. Many world leaders were convinced that the brutality and carnage of war would make men of peace, convert them to love. The man in history's streets, too, wanted to believe that victory would bring lasting peace. But real peace never comes until each man exercises his own will to be good, to love rather than to hate. Love disarms enemies at so much less cost than war! It is all but impossible to discover why man puts so much more effort into hate and death than into love and life. The evidence is overwhelming that man lacks not the intelligence but the goodwill, the love for real peace.

What is this power to love? It is the power by which a man sees the good of each other person as equal to his own, makes the good of each other person his purpose, his goal. Any particular or special love comes only from a broad base of general loving. Love, like man himself, begins small, with a gentle, outgoing interest in all the others one comes in contact with, and then spreads from a broad base of general loving until its intensity and power reach another individual in such understanding that they become one in a way far surpassing a mere physical relationship. Their minds and wills, their spirits, are one; their work, ambitions and interests are one, though each retains his individuality, his wholeness. Their union excludes no one, makes room for all who need them, who can appreciate and share the virtually inexhaustible riches they find in love.

Love can neither be legislated nor compelled, but is a person-to-person voluntary relationship. It is not necessarily a mutual relationship, though through complete misunderstanding of love, most people refuse to believe love is possible when unreturned. Love is a free man's offering of himself in service to another, regardless of whether that service is accepted or even acknowledged. Love is the power to make an outright gift, not a trade. Love given for love returned is a contradiction. Love is the ability to see and the willingness to fulfil the true needs of another *without return*. Thus the loving person is quite capable of loving the unloving as well as the loving. Love given generally does evoke love in return from those secure enough to love, but the degree of the love returned depends on the maturity of the loved one and his glad recognition of the goodness of the lover. The love relationship is neither a fifty-fifty proposition nor a two-way street. It is two one-way streets, two 100% unilateral gifts, each lover functioning independently with maximum concern for the other and minimum concern for self.

Love is the power by which man handles all situations successfully and directs all relationships for the good and happiness of other people, while respecting their freedom and integrity. It is the power by which a person is open and responsive to truth, beauty and goodness. Through it parents serve their children without spoiling them; children respond to their parents without surrendering their identity; man serves God, society, nation, neighbours and family with freedom in the process of growth. Love is the greatest quality of a real person, and the only one which can inspire and hold the love and respect of another. Love is the one thing in which disappointment is impossible. It is the unshakeable personal security which lets one invest in another without fear or loss, enables one to absorb rejection with understanding. Even in those capable of little favourable response, true love by its very generosity gradually awakens and inspires such a sense of their own power to love that they begin to look at other people in a way they have never experienced. They are like the blind given sight, looking on a new world of lovable people to be loved. The miracle of loving uncovers and enlivens the spark of self-esteem and worth in every man. Regardless of its romantic poetry and music, love is not an accident. It is the finest deliberate act of a fully responsible human being, and so, the highest tribute one person can pay to another. The power to love, put simply, is the ability to be governed in all that is thought, said or done by the best interests of others, rather than by conventions, politics, respect of person, self-interest or trade. Love is above the law, it requires the minimum because it assures the maximum. Love is not lawless but flawless.

Love is expansive and diffusive rather than exclusive and possessive. It is that quality in a person which forces its way out, seeks others, is interested in others, therefore takes the emphasis off oneself and relieves one of the miseries which come from bare existence in the prison of self-pity, anxiety and loneliness. It shares itself without being reduced, threatened or lost. It can never be restricted to or possessed by one person for it is genuinely interested in, and outgoing to, all. It is neither obstrusive nor invasive; it respects the rights and privileges of all, including their privacy. Everyone who loves has a tremendous sense of really living, of eager aliveness, of having found the purpose in life, of seeing the meaning in things. This sense is what makes it possible to absorb rejection and punishment without bitterness, to suffer while still feeling privileged. Actually, love is the quality underlying all conviction about immortality, for there is something about true love which makes it invulnerable, impervious even to death, enduring beyond any reasoned limit. Thus, loving people never run out of hope.

Man is meant to copulate because he was born with the equipment to do so. What is not so plainly obvious is that man is equally born with the equipment to think and love, and that it is as natural for him to think and to love as it is for him to copulate. Omitting for a moment the darkness of the mind and weakness of the will consequential to original sin, a child comes into the world without prejudice or scars, anxious only to get free of the womb and into the world, expecting to be well loved and cared for. If it is warmly and tenderly received it will move naturally into a loving way of life. A child is born of its first teacher, its mother, and into its first classroom, its home. Church, school and society are secondary influences however profound they may be. If the children of well-mannered, educated people are off to a first-rate academic start, the valued children of loving parents are on their way to being the best emotionally adjusted in the world.

Emotional security derives from the sense of personal worth with which a child comes into the world and which loving parents carefully nurture to maturity. Born with a basic goodness, a value, the child becomes aware of it as a sense of its own worth. It is the first thing, apart from life itself, to flourish or wither according to the environment in which it finds itself. The sense of worth will persist and thrive to the degree that the child is loved for it. It is as if a child were born into an inheritance of spiritual wealth. If real love is lavished on the child that inheritance increases in leaps and bounds. If that child senses itself to be unwanted and unloved its inheritance is so dissipated and dispersed that virtually no sense of worth remains. Deeply loving parents bring out this sense of worth in a child so strongly that it can seldom ever be lost. But unless it is brought out it is doubtful that that child will ever be a whole person or ever succeed in loving anyone well.

Social scientists have concluded that emotional health is largely determined in the first year of life. It has been generally observed that babies thrive emotionally who have been gladly breast-fed, because loving attention is their earliest experience, which registers primarily, of course, in their feelings. Emphasis should be on the "gladly" rather than "breast-fed" because grudging breast feeding by selfish, uninterested mothers is less desirable than interested bottle feeding by nurses. The point is that when the breasts are gladly used for the function for which they are designed the infant gets the message clearly that it is loved and wanted, it receives loving interest which it is being very much emotionally conditioned to return just as gladly.

The basic ability to love is seen in the early capacity to be interested in others. That interest is the broad base of loving without which the potential to love would not develop. Every encour-

agement should be given children to go out to others, to cooper
ate with them and contribute to their best interests. This is the
actual disposition of the child warmly received into a loving home.
This child will not be thrown off by fear of a rejection it has not
experienced in infancy.

Because God is Love, there are hardly more hypocritical words
than "I love you" used to prove devotion to another while exploiting that person for one's own satisfaction. "I love you" are words
almost universally used to express physical, sexual attraction to
someone, the desire to possess that person sexually as soon as possible. As mouthed by so many, they signify so much greater desire
to take than to give that even children quickly recognize the hy-
pocrisy in them. They are used hypocritically by parents to im-
pose their wills on their children, to compel affection, to beg tol
erance, or to project their own ambitions on their children. They
are used in turn by the children to bribe or seduce their parents
into gifts, or to insinuate their own wills. They are used, with incredible shallowness, in the entertainment and commerical worlds
for the benefit of those who pay the most. They are used by citizens in general to protest their love of country, always used loud-
est when there is least demand on them personally and the greatest benefit from merely being citizens. What "I love you" really
ought to mean is "You are of the highest importance to me. Your
welfare has high priority in my life. I respect you as I respect
myself. I will share not only my possessions with you, but my life."
Obviously, whoever can tell another he loves, and be speaking the
truth, is as superb as he is rare.

Despite the use of love in reference to God, neighbours, parents
children, brothers and sisters, and even native country, many people today still automatically assume that sex and love are one. One
result of this is that, since sex is easy, love is likewise assumed to
be easy. Love also seems deceptively easy because it is so readily
confused with falling or being "in love", an emotional state of
euphoria, delight. The emotions of love and the delights of sexual
pleasure, purely personal sensations, are to most people the only
infallible signs of deep personal love. Those who have fallen in
love two or three times know perfectly well that the delightful
expectations of a deep personal relationship to follow are generally empty and unwarranted ones. Highly charged, emotional be-

ginnings seldom stand the test of time and generally lead nowhere. Sex requires only the most superficial of relationships, with very quickly reached physical limits. Love is a relationship of unlimited depth, innumerable ramifications revealing the persons involved to each other indefinitely in new ways and depths.

One who settles for genital pleasure as an end in itself writes off the happiness of love. However great the undoubted pleasure of sex, the purely mechanicl functions of the genital organs can never be a high human achievement. Sex feelings do give the impetus to relate to another person but they are merely occasions, never causes of, a loving relationship. Personal reform stimulated by sex is never improvement but mere accommodation, self-interested adaption. Sex is dependent entirely on the feelings, whereas love is a willed giving and caring, often with, but not dependent on love feelings. Man is born with both the equipment required for sex and the potential to love but he must acquire the goodwill and virtue to integrate his sex into his life of love and so to be a better person himself and contribute to the personal growth of the one he loves.

Love is bigger even than death. Death never ends true love, and this makes it possible for men to die in peace. Those who love through death discover in subsequent love not the fickle replacement of a dead love but an enrichment of life made possible by an earlier love. Sex, on the other hand, barely endures through the emotional *now*.

Those who insist that man is a man only if he copulates, make manhood's qualifications pretty meagre. The man who does not love, whether he copulates or not, is much less a man. Sexual activity in itself does not express personal interest, understanding, companionship, mutual tolerance, support or inspiration, all qualities surpassing the purely sexual potential. Although the spirituality of sex is lost in removing sex from love, the humanity of sex is lost by removing love from sex. The more indispensable the sexual union the less vital the personal union, though the love bond is stronger because of the happily accepted sexual polarity. No deep friendship can exist when the sexual dimension is ignored, but it also doesn't exist when a relationship is purely sexual. Sex, which is personally destructive as a dominating force, reaches its perfection in the love-dominated person. People whose communication is limited to sexual intercourse soon have little in common and nothing to say to each other. The blind acceptance that sex is bigger than the person makes love impossible. Those who cannot wait until marriage to share their sexual lives, are writing off the loving life on which a happy marriage depends. Sex, which can contribute much to love, is never allowed to deprive wise or good people of the love which gives the meaning to sex, in fact, its humanity.

Love must be learned, it does not come automatically, however natural it is to man. Love certainly can be taught—in fact, deserves full status as a science, something to be studied, learned, understood and done. As one can be taught, though not made, to think, one can be taught, though not made, to love. But the power to love is in every human being and the best teachers should be trained and provided to teach love, because the future of man depends, under God, entirely on the exercise of his power to love.

CHAPTER EIGHT

The High Cost of Unloving

Man must await history's verdict on the present. Is it the beginning of the great decline, the decay of Western civilization, or merely the herald of a new puritanism, a revolt against man's own excesses, especially his sexual excesses? Certainly it is the age of the Great Sexual Hoax, for never has sex been so commercialized. The masses are being gladly conned into believing that they are living in a time of great enlightenment, a new understanding of sex, the age of freedom blessed by technological development to give the time and leisure needed for pure enjoyment. Man feels himself on the very threshhold of his own heaven on earth, pure pleasure on his own terms. Many, however, are having misgivings, haunting doubts intruding on them just when they thought they had it made. There are stupid, narrow-minded bigots abroad, spoilers who have lost faith in man, who refuse to accept without question that he can build and enjoy the world of his own options. There are war, inflation, poverty, hunger, disease, pollution, crime, addiction, energy crisis, taxes, and innumerable other ugly things that just will not go away. These phenomena can make almost anyone doubt, even while standing on the very brink of the golden age of total pleasure. Only the envied swinger winging his way from one privilege to another without touching a single obligation would like us to believe that he has all the answers. Yet even he knows better; he does not dare take time to think. Man, making new troubles faster by far than he can solve them, is getting more and more frightened. And with good reason.

Man's current preoccupation is with his sexual life. Love is made easy by limiting it to copulation, which has little if anything to do with love and so very much to do with exploitation. Man rather envies the apes because, although there is no love in their lives, there seems to be plenty of unruffled copulation. Lucky apes —no love, no sex hangups, pure copulation, a rather simple and enjoyable thing. Man, on the other hand, does have sex hangups, but only because in everything he does he can love, even in copulation. When man's copulation is not loving, something always goes wrong. It puzzles man that he cannot copulate without restraint and still be loving. He insists that his hangups must come from the mechanics of the thing rather than the nature of the man. It must be that he just does not know how to do it well. So he registers in a "how-to" school, one of those human zoos where they teach a man to copulate like the apes to get the highest possible pleasure from his efforts, something the apes do quite easily without ever going to school. After graduation many people really enjoy copulation, because they have become very good at it. They can do everything the manuals said to do. But they cannot love. That is not in the manuals; it is not the reason they went to school. They went to the "how-to" school for their own sake. Love, for too many, makes copulation very difficult, if not impossible; love requires that even copulation be for the good of others. That is the reason love is as difficult as it is rewarding.

In teaching people how to copulate well, the sexual liberators tell them how important it is to their health to enjoy themselves. A man who could laugh would catch on quite easily that he was being had. The teacher's first love is not really pleasure or copulation but money; his motive is not sex but greed. Just as the prostitute loves money and an easy life more than she does sex, so many sexologists find the monetary rewards more than adequate for their efforts on behalf of those who insist so wrongly that sex is all-important. Art, drama, music, literature, journalism, philosophy, psychology, medicine—almost every phase of modern living has been prostituted to money through sex. All in the name of "the good life", of course!

As anyone who ever saw a naked man and woman can easily guess, they fit together physically; they have complementary genitals. Furthermore, both are naturally equipped with the basic desire to use them. But what is much less evident yet far more meaningful is that as people, persons, they fit together too, and what they need and want ever so much more than sex is a deep, true, lasting relationship in love. And this, which is what human living is all about, does not so much bring them pleasure as happiness, something remarkably missing in modern luxury living. Man's happiness never comes from someone else but originates deep within himself when he is functioning as a human being should, when he is loving. If man will stop worrying about *premarital sex* and concentrate on *premarital love* a giant step will indeed have been taken for mankind, greater progress than through any technological discovery, the very step that could give meaning to progress.

Because man can do anything he chooses to do lovingly, he can copulate lovingly. Everyman begins life through an act of copulation (so generally, if incorrectly, called love). However dim the spark of love in this act may be—the merest blip in the dark storm of lust, or a glorious burst of blinding light—the potential for love is conceived by it. Corded to his placental lifepack, foetal man fights for nine months to be free to live his own life. After his struggle from the protective capsule of the womb he greedily grasps the breasts he needs so desperately. No matter how hard he struggles he can never be truly free of others, from whom he must receive, as indeed to whom he in turn must give. Even when he is physically mature and self-reliant, emotionally he still reaches for the breast, which nourishing him discovers the warmth of being needed, and even more—understanding, companionship, inspiration and love.

And so while man must understand all that is specifically human about the act by which he is conceived, it is even more important that he grasp that he is born to love and find happiness by doing so, or be destined to hate and die, not once in physical death, but daily in hating everyone and everything around him. A very high price indeed a man pays for unloving. The price to be paid for the happiness of loving is not small; it was described, by One who claimed to know, as losing oneself to find oneself. The price of loving is to give love top priority in life, with much later and less consideration to things like riches, fame, power and pleasure. Settling for less has left people so obviously miserable, even in the affluent world where things surely have priority over people. But the price of unloving is inestimable.

The man who rejects his tremendous potential for happiness in loving must experience the terrible consequences of unloving. They are as clear as they are unpleasant. Addictions, crime, violence, hate and war on a scale not dreamed of, made inconceivably horrendous by advanced technology, rejecting all restraints by or direction from love, are the immediate ones. Man's intelligence is a disaster when he refuses to be good. However, the obvious cost of unloving, in the affluent society, is the loneliness so evident everywhere.

Loneliness is a long-lasting, devastating experience which everyone dreads, but few do much about. Man has moved so intelligently into less serious problems that it is beyond belief that he does so little about this one. The same diligent effort he has undertaken so often, applied to loneliness, would quickly bring the cure. The antidote for loneliness is loving. Not in being loved, but in positively loving others. In loving, man quickly discovers the cure for all psychosomatic disorders, the power he has to put his mind on someone other than himself. Loneliness is only a symptom of a malfunctioning will, and can be remedied by understanding love and acquiring the discipline, the virtue, to love. The poor, downtrodden, hungry and seriously ill do not feel loneliness much because of the more urgent and immediate pressures on them. The full impact of loneliness is felt predominantly by the materially successful, the affluent, who are aware of having everything except what matters most, love. Worldly success comes to most people through their ability and willingness to exploit others, the very process which breeds loneliness. It is being unloving rather than being unloved which causes loneliness.

Love is the power to invest oneself in others, in people rather than in things. Few of those so anxious to get, receive, have or possess are willing to lift a finger to love, because love has such low priority in their lust for power or for material things. Achievers worship success, almost purely material in their eyes. Having met the requirements of an academic-oriented society, they simply do not believe in a love they made no time for, which could only be an obstacle to their getting ahead. Love's magic escapes them until it is too late. Filled with the frustrations inseparable from success, and the contempt they have for those they have so easily exploited, idols in the midst of worshippers of the material, they are doomed to enjoy only a purchased love. They are victims of every kind of psychosomatic disease (their bodies have been so carefully cared for while their souls were starved); their doctors live off their illnesses. Hospitals are their houses of prostitution where they pay grudgingly for the purchased love to which they are addicted. Their psychiatrists and counselors are their fantasy lovers; the shallow, porcelain-cold, casual kiss of greeting at a door the warmest affection in their lives. When they cannot have whatever they want, they suffer withdrawal symptoms, emotional tantrums of one kind or another. Their power to love is cut off by their irresistible desire to be loved for what they are, even when they are obviously nothing. They die by inches of the cancer of addiction to themselves. The fulfilment in loving escapes them completely; their lifelong habit of dishonesty has cut them off, long ago, from the honest who alone could love them. As long as the eternal question is "What is in it for me?" the answer must inevitably remain, "Nothing, of course." Nothing is always the return on an investment never made.

The high cost of unloving, almost beyond reckoning, begins with the refusal to use one's basic capacity for real interest in others. That unused power inevitably turns to resentment, hate and corruption. The mercenary preoccupation of the news media with sex, crime, violence and corruption illustrates the ease with which genuine interest in others becomes morbid curiosity, shows how the exploitation of the misdeeds and misfortunes of others stimulates the sick delight in the unloving man who relishes the degrading exposure of the sins and weaknesses of his brother, as he gloats with feelings of relief and superiority. Such people all but demand, and the press goes to endless lengths to provide, the gory details of their neighbours' most revolting misadventures. The fantastic appetite for gossip, intrigue, character assassination, and the reduction of the high and mighty to less than life size, is indisputable evidence of interest perverted. People who would not develop the interest which in the beginning was genuine and efficacious, and could have led to love, everywhere excuse the worst in themselves by piously pointing to those who are more wicked than they. Those who, in their greed for riches and power, exploit the greed and corruption of the poor, who deplore the costs to themselves of a just society, pay vastly more for the protection of a tyranny dedicated to containing anarchy, to carrying on business as usual.

The honest, loving man contends with himself squarely and

courageously. The dishonest, unloving man blames everyone else for his troubles, which multiply in direct proportion to his frustrations. History is a scathing record of the untapped potential for love flooding into destructive channels. The sordid record of hate makes it difficult to believe that the power of love is really greater. Hate is the alternative to love. It is the active refusal to respond to, and embrace, the good, ending in a determined effort to destroy the good. Real power is in the hands only of those who love or hate. The masses, in varying stages of indifference, bore themselves to death as addicts in pursuit of pleasure, or flight from pain, living on the fringes of love or hate, while the lovers and the haters make the future. War, mass hate, would seem to be reason enough to persuade anyone to love, yet peace has generally meant to the unloving masses merely the opportune leisure to resume their unimpeded exploitation of others. Protests against war are patently false when the protesters are not prepared to love. They are generally protesting only the interruption of their pleasures. Typically the unloving man looks for an easier road to peace than by confronting the truth which makes love possible. He wants to have his cake and eat it too. He will fight the man who takes him from the vomit of his choice.

The unloving man constantly runs through the litany of devils which make him unhappy—the establishment, the economic system, cultural heritage, skin pigment, unequal treaties, power blocs, the military-industrial complex, everything but himself. He screams, "make love, not war," a beautiful slogan for those really prepared to love, but completely phoney when mouthed by those replacing the mass exploitation of war with the personal exploitation of irresponsible sex. To love, one must at least be winning the battle for possession of oneself, one must have acquired at least sufficient discipline to equate the good of another with one's own.

Crime is one man's war on himself, his neighbour and society. It is one man blowing his personal integrity for thirty pieces of silver. Gangsters, rioters, mobs, anarchists signify a sick society unequal to loving. Hate breeds hate. Violence, however understandable and seemingly commendable, merely replaces one tyranny with another. Genuine freedom is possible only where there is genuine love. Emerging races or nations simply pass from the jungle of ignorance to the jungle of exploitation, simply surrender one form of slavery for another, unless they weld loving to their learning and technology.

Every form of pollution is increased evidence of the high cost of unloving, the perverse destruction of the things man should love most and conserve. The lover alone accuses himself first and sees unloving as, essentially, man's pollution of himself. A little humour, which every unloving person lacks, would reveal the ridiculous stance of the man railing against air pollution as he stands censoriously glaring at an industrial smokestack, with a cigarette in his hand. Addicts can remain addicts only as long as they deny the obvious pollution of themselves by their own addictions. Man has little respect for nature when he has none for himself, when he blindly lays waste his fantastic power to love. His power to control nature is a bad joke if he will not control himself; true birth control surely must be seen first as self-control. Unloving is the rejection of personal discipline.

Emotional domination, the basis of addiction, must be added to the cost of unloving. The enlightened discernment and disciplined good judgment coming from love enables one to treat one's fellow man properly regardless of one's feelings. Great lovers can treat enemies with justice and decency. They alone can bring peace to the world, which prays for peace in vain unless it also loves. Emotionally dominated people can neither listen nor ponder. Easily aroused, they are generally in turmoil or complete withdrawal. Insecure, easily threatened and frightened, they react immediately to what is filtered through their overriding emotions before they can even try to understand its real significance. The material of the senses is distorted by their twisted emotions, sending out alarms which create panic. They never really communicate. Their dialogues are "duologues"—two people talking, neither listening. For them to love means the desire to possess—understanding means agreement, helping another means getting their own way; raising children well means fulfilling themselves. Flattery is truth for them and jealousy the highest form of flattery. Their loveless marriages and hopeless homes are part of the high cost of unloving which, through emotional inflation, spawns the crippled tyrants who hate so well, and the cop-out parasites of society.

All addiction—to food or drink, to money, power, sex, or drugs

—is slavery to self, man defaulting completely in the face of pleasant or unpleasant reality. The addict with sufficient honesty to blame himself for his addiction is half cured. There is some hope that despite every bad influence in his life—derelict parents, bad companions, poverty and suffering—he will discover the secret of happiness in his own power to love. The most stupid thing man can do is blame God and religion rather than himself for the strife and turmoil existing everywhere in the world, and use this excuse for seeking the hopeless shelter of addiction. The greatest hypocrites are the myopic scientists claiming utter objectivity in their search for truth, while rejecting the God of truth, beauty and goodness. Only the sick and selfish could smugly close their eyes to the human wreckage from pleasure addiction and the emotional binge which their "objective norms" have strewn around, more painfully obvious than the ruins of all the wars.

CHAPTER NINE

The Loving Life

The loving life is man at his best, so relating to others that he shares with them, to the fullest extent, all that he is and has. Before anyone loves deeply, he must accept man's inherent power to love; he must believe that God endowed man with such a potential. Belief in one's fellow man, which is the basis of love, lies in the conviction that, however undeveloped, that power is there awaiting awakening by the loving of others. Those who refuse to accept this inherent power, and the obligation of using it for the development and growth of their fellow men, will use their own power to love in exploiting others for pleasure or other self-oriented purposes.

My loving life begins when I learn to take an interest in each and every person I come in contact with, and my potential to love develops accordingly as I allow myself to be absorbed and fulfilled in those loving associations. I do not learn to love by singling out one person who interests or attracts me because that person represents something I need or want. Rather, in going out to all others around me according to *their* needs, I discover any number of interesting people who respond to my interest and from among these I become aware of someone of such truth and beauty that a deeper relationship develops which is distinguished by its diffusive goodness. Out of a broad unselective experience of society come the deep, loving personal relationships characteristic of the loving life at its best, its most fruitful, its summit.

My loving interest is clearly shown by being what I can be to others and doing what I can do for others according to their needs, and to the opportunities provided and the resources available. I do not put people into my debt, nor do I create a personality cult. My interest is not selective or discriminatory, but given where necessary and possible. However casual it may be—and it always begins casually—it must be always personal and genuine, rather than vague and contrived. My interest is restricted neither to equals, to inferiors, nor to superiors, but extends to all. It has the faculty of, and facility in, establishing a working equality with negligible sense of obligation or indebtedness, but a great sense of privilege. It is gracious rather than bountiful.

Man's survival depends on love to eliminate the exploitation passing for love in the lives of so many people. Love makes learning meaningful. Lacking love, academic learning must be oriented to pride, greed and self. Education has given man so many things he enjoys. However, he will lose them unless he shares them. The efficacious theology of affluence and sharing can show new nations that education without love is an avoidable disaster for man.

Prosperity has nothing but disillusionment to offer materialists, who see less and less to struggle for. As affluent America has grown richer and better fed, clothed and housed, she has become more corrupt, lazy, uninterested and selfish. People need to share their good things with others in love. Sharing offers something as essential to the benefactor as to the beneficiary. For much too long man's acknowledged needs have been material and physical, rather than spiritual and personal. Whoever dreamed up the delusion that the gospel cannot be preached to people with empty stomachs, obviously never tried to preach the gospel to people with full stomachs, whose fatty tissue so conveniently plugs their ears, insulating them from the truth. The poor and hungry people listen to the gospel because God is their only hope. They are too painfully aware that their fellow man could hardly care less about them. People with available resources seldom live with an awareness of their dependence on God; people who are physically comfortable tend to forget the spiritual. And love is spiritual, it is a power, an intangible, impressive both in what it is and in what it does. Love eludes those who are more impressed by what they have than by what they are.

The loving life is a whole person, aware of his dignity, worth and responsibility, living equally with his fellow man. The power to love enables a man to rise above his personal needs, which he readily equates with those of others and sacrifices for the common good. He achieves this life when he accepts that people are more important than things. Man gives many years of his early life to academic studies because his material progress requires it. He gives precious little time or thought to loving because he understands his physical well-being so much better than he appreciates growth as a person. Hopefully, as he now surveys the human wreckage around him, the mounting evidence of chronic unhappiness everywhere in the highly developed nations, he may be moved by the calamitous effects of unloving, the personal emptiness of his life, to set earnestly about the task of loving. The desperate need of the civilized world for the loving redemption of its technology is daily more apparent. The world's enthusiasm for loving must, at least, equal its enthusiasm for learning. The most primitive emerging nations now willingly budget for the education of their people because their proper development depends on it. They must understand and avoid the mistake of the industrial giants in letting love lag so far behind learning that progress is neutralized by unhappiness. The Church, which in the Western world pioneered so effectively in academic learning, must now turn its full attention and efforts to loving, the basic Christian commitment.

To achieve the loving life, man must accept that to remain unloving is to remain half developed, only half human. Not the unloved, but the unloving, fails as a person. How else explain the numbers of lonely people living in wealth? People with every material comfort remain desperate for fulfilment, for meaning in their still empty lives. They have tried every substitute for love — money, sex, prestige, drugs, and even the last desperate answer of all, the ultimate cop-out — suicide. How obviously only love is missing! How ridiculous not to give it a try! However poetical or ideal it sounds, the "I-thou" loving relationship is the reason for man's deep joy and happiness, his essential growth as a person. The "I-thou" loving relationship preserves man from addictions, to self, sex, drugs, food, drink and superstition. It liberates him from fear of pain, sorrow and sickness. Man prefers many things before love only because he is stupid or sick. So monstrous is his ego that he prefers his own judgment to God's, which is what sin is about. To avoid the calamity of unloving, man need only ask someone who has deeply loved whether love was wasted, regretted, or in any way a source of unhappiness. The answer would be clear enough. Unfortunately, each man has to learn for himself.

The difference between real love and its many cheap imitations is in the certain, deep and lasting happiness that real love assures.

Man wants to love. The desire to love is built into him; love is an essential function for him. It is the most personal thing in his life. It cannot be done for him. He cannot be made to love. He has to choose, to will to do it. The loving life, however, is beyond one who confuses fulfilment with reward. Man is fulfilled when he functions as a man, that is, when he loves. He is rewarded when he is loved, which is something which can depend only indirectly on him, and for which he cannot be responsible. The truly loving person cannot be lured into loving by rewards, because he knows his fulfilment lies in his own positive loving. Among the immediate fruits of the loving life are true friendship, genuine community spirit, honest affection, meaningful courtship. These things are generated by people whose security and deep peace enable their love to manifest itself, without reserve, in genuine and efficacious interest in others.

All the above effects sound like tired clichés. They have great meaning, and yet convey an inescapable triteness which does not communicate their significance. Still, one can only try to express the rich meaning of those words, however threadbare abuse has made them. Man is a social animal, so friendship is vital. Yet, the larger the number of friends claimed, the less the word friendship really means. Most people are so anxious to prove their irresistibility that they speak of the most casual acquaintances as friends. Realists speak of real friends in ones or twos. Anything more and they really mean community, a mutually interested and motivated group, not primarily friends. A real friend will immediately, at serious inconvenience to himself, willingly assist his friend in difficulty, not once or twice but as often as necessary, at any time. A friend is one with whom a person can be open, unafraid of exposure or rejection—in other words, secure.

The outstanding factor in friendship is the ability to communicate. To communicate one must be understanding, have some very real conviction, have awareness of and interest in others, and believe that one can open not one's body, but one's deepest self, to the other. Love makes the inevitable risk acceptable. The test of friendship between male and female is the love that outweighs sex, possessions, position or any emotional domination. To put it simply, friendship gives top priority to the good of the friend.

Community is the magic word. Yet only people who actually love can generate community. Community is not something one lives on but something one contributes to. Community is not built from crumbling bricks. It is totally defeated by people wanting privileges without accepting obligations, people who will not pay the bills. In real community the love of the strong sparks the weak to make them contributors; it raises them to life as only the miracle of love can. Community is not a group of parasites but an association of people of some goodwill, loving people. Unloving people drain community of its vitality. The corporate group gets hope from the resources of the group. The bond between the members is love or it is delusion. The idea that members can be compelled rather than inspired to measure up is ridiculous.

The place of affection in the loving life is specific, and important. The necessity and role of affection should not be lightly overlooked or dismissed. Affection is like money; it has a real value which few use well. It can provide for or corrupt, assist or seduce. Needless to say, it is honest affection that is meant. Honest affection is the deliberate manifestation of feelings in a responsible relationship of true love, understood correctly by both persons in the relationship, never threatening but always contributing to its growth. It is as wrong to deprive loved ones of honest affection as it is to express dishonest affection. Genuine affection has been too generally suppressed because too much dishonest affection is too easily expressed. The manner and degree of the affection expressed depend entirely on the good of the people involved. That is to say, it is always given and received in the context of one's commitments and intentions. For example, the affection of married people is extended to others within the limits of their marriage commitment; parents are not incestuous; celibate affection is not genitally geared. True affection is never an occasion of hardship, confusion or serious emotional upset to anyone involved. Affection can be a nod, a smile, or a knowing look and may go on to a holding of hands, a hug, a kiss or other endearment which has a real message of genuine loving interest but is never attempted seduction. In genuine loving relationships none of these actions need cause genital sex arousal, though, of course, they can be used for this purpose, or can be mistaken as being intended for this purpose. To say that such honest affection is impossible or wrong is merely to insist that love is impossible.

Because of the traditional suspicion of affection it can be very disconcerting to the good people best qualified to give and receive it. This is mainly because of the accompanying sexual emotions which, if understood, are very helpful in gauging the acceptable intensity of its expression. These feelings, in themselves, are never reason to suppress affection. Affection shown should truly represent and be understood for what it is—the manifestation of a special, personal, loving relationship. The secondary sexual element in all affection is normal and healthy. However, the honest affection of mature people is of a personal, not a sexual, significance. It never has primary sexual overtones. Thus, honest affection inevitably results in both people being better people, more relaxed, secure, open to, and understanding of each other, more interested in, useful and available to others. Good people who have no one with whom to be themselves, or to whom they can reveal themselves, tend to crack up.

In contrast, affection which results in sexual frustration, exclusiveness, possessiveness (not in feelings only but in fact), lessening of dedication and chronic discontent with life, all characteristics of emotionally dominated people—such affection is always dishonest. Inadequate people are devastated by feigned affection simulating exclusive friendship. They generally misinterpret even the affection displayed as routine common courtesy. Misused affection leaves scars as deep as brutality; it makes emotional cripples. Honest affection is displayed in attitude, interest, word and action; it is stimulated by friendship, the ability of friends to communicate and understand, and other similar factors.

Courtship is a circumstance of special love and friendship. There is then a specific relationship in which both people honestly expect marriage to eventuate. There is both more reason for expressed affection, and a much greater danger of self-deception and dishonesty. The great tendency and danger is to justify the present manifestations of affection by an uncertain future relationship which simply cannot justify them, instead of being sure that they are restricted to the realities of the relationship present here and now. The very honesty which rejects the exploitation so understandable in courtship is the quality which indicates responsible maturity and real hope of love in the possible future relationship. Courtship is undeniably the greatest opportunity to learn the discipline required by love in a happy marriage, *e.g.*, the discipline required for fidelity, good management, responsible parenthood. It foresees almost every difficulty to be encountered in marriage, and should be a time of deep understanding and thoughtful concern, rather than of wishful thinking and mirages.

True interest in the welfare of the loved permits loving people to enjoy courtships, and prevents those courtships from being traumas of emotional desire and possessiveness, in which the lust for sexual fulfilment obliterates all real hope of personal relationship.

The sexual intercourse which is of such high excitement in courtship almost inevitably becomes a bore in marriage. Only interesting people can keep sex from becoming a bore. Love makes courtship a process of personal discovery quite within the capability of those genuinely interested in others, though quite beyond those who can't face themselves, let alone expose themselves to the discerning scrutiny of another. Love is the power not to be sidetracked in courtship by any lesser dimension than the personal, so that the courtship actually leads to a marriage in which the sexual sharing is enjoyed in the context of the personal love. Marriage should take place between people already loving, who have successfully negotiated the risks in learning to love. To make modern courtship an emotional standoff of immature people in a highly explosive situation is to assure the destruction of marriage as an institution. The loving life equips people for responsible courtship, which is true courtship rather than trial marriage, or more correctly, trial sex. When the interest of people in each other peaks in a sex-oriented courtship, a tragic marriage generally follows in which one or both parties soon abandon any honest effort to love.

CHAPTER TEN

Learning to Love.

It is difficult to deal separately with the next three chapters—Learning to Love, The Personal Relationship, and Premarital Love—because they are so closely related in so many aspects. However the emphasis is quite distinct. To begin with the first, there are many prejudices against the very thought of learning to love. Not only do people want to believe that love just happens, but there is a general tendency to restrict learning to an academic process, a course or term, which when finished has had the desired result. Yet love is something one learns from life rather than in school, and though there are many important and interesting facts related to loving that one can study, love is not a matter of facts or even study, but of personal growth and experience.

Love is something that ought to be begun very young but that continues right through life. There is no resting on one's laurels or standing still. There is no point in life at which one can say he has arrived, he knows all there is to know about love. Although academic courses in the subject, if available, could have much of value to offer, and although the understanding and experience of others in loving could be presented for helpful consideration, learning to love is a way of life. The work of the poets, the definitions of the psychologists and the profundities of the philosophers are of little help in learning to love without the individual applying himself to love in his personal life, the task for which he was born. He must be convinced that the meaning in his life is to be found only through his loving—the central, specifically human function that gives the only true significance to his every act.

Unfortunately, too, in our culture, to speak of love immediately conjures up the vision of boy meets girl, the male-female coupling.

Yet, in fact, this so called love, originates much more in the mating bond than the love bond. While the naturalists ponder the instincts and behaviour of animals because they can, though not necessarily do, cast light on human behaviour, it must be admitted that man does share the mating instinct with the beasts. Man is born into the world with genitals, and with that equipment comes the desire to use it. However, the equipment and desire have nothing to do directly with loving. Man's mating is as loving or unloving as he is as a person. Furthermore, the female has the nesting instinct. With all due respect to her liberation, woman, for reasons too varied to catalogue or describe, has the desire for a home, or nest, into which she can place her offspring. This instinct, far more often than love, propels her to acquire a husband and provider. While most married people in our times and culture believe, simply because they want to believe it, that they marry because of love, they generally marry because they want each other rather than love each other. Love has precious little to do with getting what one wants but everything to do with sharing what one has and is. Thus when one has presumed that he is already loving, he has little inclination to learn to love.

In a society that is prejudiced in favour of calling the sexual relationship love, when it is not, there is equal prejudice against using the term "love" between two men or two women because of the "homosexual" overtones. But there are neither sexual nor homosexual tones or overtones to the word "love", which is strictly a relationship between people, between persons. It is certainly a great prejudice against learning to love to have given the whole matter of loving such sexual overtones that one almost instinctively denies this basic truth about loving, that there is only one kind of human love. One loves or he does not. He is never a lover of some and hater of others. As a matter of fact, no one loves another any more or less than he loves God, mother or father, brothers or sisters, sons or daughters, or neighbours. Love is not different in each case because manifested in a different way or relationship, or experienced to a different degree. To repeat, one either loves or he does not. When he loves, it is with all the understanding, interest, concern and devotion of which he is capable in the circumstances in which he finds himself. Because one has never met a person does not mean that he does not love that person or have any interest in him. It simply means that there has been no occasion to bring that love to bear in a relationship. But it is there should the relationship become a reality.

Materialistic man hardly considers love apart from dimensions he can see or touch. He expects to love without knowing its nature or substance. This makes love extremely difficult. Love does not just happen; it is achieved and perfected by practice, by living it. It is then that man is mature.

It should be obvious that love is not a sexual thing for the simple reason that people usually mature sexually between the ages of eleven and sixteen, long before they are capable of mature and meaningful love. If loving were synonymous with sex, one would be as ready for it at twelve to sixteen years of age as at any time. Yet one has not matured physically before 21 to 25 years of age, and emotional maturity which is required for mature love, comes well after physical maturity. Only the loving person can be called personally mature, for only when he is actually loving deeply and well can he be said to be doing the thing for which he is alive or created. One has acquired a great deal of wisdom before one is mature. Both the wisdom to make good decisions and the virtue it takes to implement them, both in one's own case and in the interests of others, are qualities of the mature person. It can be safely said that most people are not personally mature, that is genuinely loving, before they are forty to fifty years of age. Unhappily, too many people live and die without ever having reached a point at which it can be truthfully said of them that they are indeed deeply and personally loving. Learning to love is the only thing that can bring them to that stage, however long it takes. Needless to say, the younger it starts the better off they are.

There is no better start in learning to love than being born of loving parents into a loving home. The advantages of such a child over the average child is easily glimpsed by a comparison in academic education. The child of native college graduates has a very real advantage over the child of foreign language immigrants of a different cultural background. The former is familiar with cultural usages and conventions from his earliest recollections. His vocabulary is greater, his interest keener, and his awareness sharper. He has many fewer mistakes to unlearn. Surely the same thing can be said of the child born of loving parents into the loving home. He has a tremendous head start. The less fortunate child is not irremediably impeded or impaired. Despite his poor start and acquired handicaps when he is awakened to love, its necessity and place of importance in life, he can achieve excellence in it proportionate to his will to achieve and ability to sacrifice for it.

Pain and pleasure are facts of life, and very fundamental ones indeed. However, they are merely qualities of experience that are acceptable or unacceptable according to their role in the desirable end to be achieved. Certainly only one who can handle both pain and pleasure well will ever be emotionally mature enough to love well. Before science had made available such insight into pain and pleasure as is needed to handle them well, strong people placed undue value on pain and undue suspicion on pleasure. Their native wisdom told them it was important to handle pain well because anyone who could do so would hardly be seduced by pleasure or crumble easily under life's difficulties. However, with the widespread availability of pain-killing drugs, there began a general flight from pain, regardless of whether it was necessary and inescapable or not. And certainly there is necessary and inescapable pain involved in loving. It is the penchant for flight from pain that has led to the widespread fear of the rejection involved in any human encounter. One tends now only to relate to those of whom one has little or no fear of rejection. So love dies aborning. If one is to relate lovingly to others, if one is to learn to love, one has to be sure there are far worse things in life than pain; one surely cannot be a fugitive from pain or an addict of pleasure. Certainly no such people, dominated as they are by what they feel, can have as their chief concern the real good of another, which is what love is all about. Fundamental to the learning to love therefore, is practice in coming to grips with the very real and limited dimensions of pain and pleasure. In loving, any pain however distressing, is acceptable or unacceptable according to its necessity and helpfulness; any pleasure, however seductive and enjoyable, is resistible if it threatens the good of the ones loved. Need it be repeated that loving demands great wisdom and strength of character, which are merely other names for virtue?

Having faced some of the basic obstacles to loving, one is confronted with the final and fundamental one. One has to decide just what it means to love and what priority it must be given in life. If we accept the earlier definition that love is the power we have to see and fulfil the true needs of another, it is obvious that we cannot be interested in the good of another if we do not have some clear ideas about what is good for ourselves, a clear set of values and priorities. If we have these, then our power to love motivates us to take whatever steps, at whatever cost, to provide these values, to whatever extent possible, for another. This is what learning to love involves. Surely no one is going to take this seriously until and unless he has finally decided that loving is what life is all about, that love and only love gives life its fundamental significance. Any effective learning to love flows from these convictions and motives. Whoever denies this, as anyone is quite free to do, can only find out that life makes little or no sense on any other basis.

Many people who undertake to love because they conclude that love is what life is all about encounter insurmountable problems because they undertake to love so that they will be what they should be, while making their efforts depend on the emotional satisfaction or feedback they receive. This process defeats itself because of diminishing returns. One who offers genuine love does not depend on the emotional feedback, but does what he does because it ought to be done. He then discovers what every lover finds out, that genuine love does bring a return many times its own size as long as it is not an investment made for the sake of the return. Love is always a gift, freely given. It is never an investment. Only free giving evokes free response. Anything else is a demand or a bribe quite at variance with genuine love. When one has learned that, one has started to love in earnest. Such love bears fruit in steadfastness, and tranquility with the ability to accept and absorb rejection and to see the rejector as the sick patient rather than the rejectee as victim. There is no escaping this learning process in the course of growth.

For the over-eager but unwary, there are traps in such a process. One of them is the temptation to invite rejection as a proof of one's superiority and loving character. That, of course, is a delusion. However, it is not much worse a delusion than the tendency to suppress the emotions to avoid feeling the pain of rejection. The one who learns to love well learns to live his or her life with the full and healthy pressure of emotions, emotions that are felt but which are never the decisive factor in the decisions to be made. The loving person bases those decisions on real values, principles and convictions that can stand the test of rejection and feels genuine pity for the cripple who rejects, who is the loser. It is very difficult to see how anyone can become this strong or this good without a deep faith in God, genuine belief in himself and so, the ability to believe in the potential of others to love. Such people can demand of themselves that they love; they never demand it of others.

It can be expected that people in a world more concerned about smelling bad than being bad, so much more interested in what they are getting out of life than what they are putting into life, would not take kindly to the chore of learning to love. That chore requires greater respect in people for their inner resources than their outer or material resources, more interest in the people they are than in the appearances they present. They have to give their minds and their wills at least equal concern with their bodies, to be as aware of spiritual neglect as of physical hunger. (So many overweight people don't realize that they are mistaking empty lives for empty stomachs). Their lives must be governed by what is good and right rather than the pressure to conform or to please others, or the "image" society demands of them. They must be quick to see what experience confirms, that what is right works, what is wrong does not. They must value personal strength over physical strength and appreciate just how much of the latter comes from the former. Such people see the "quality of life" as stemming from what a person is rather than from what a person has.

Loving must be seen not as something that two people do but rather as something that each person does. It must be accepted that it has nothing directly to do with either sex or marriage, but which, when and as achieved, flows into every aspect of human living. It is the one quality of a person that directs all his thoughts words and actions, every aspect of his personal relationships. It surely must be obvious, then, that loving is beyond someone or anyone with a low self-image or sense of worth. Learning to love never requires the surrender of one's integrity. A deep appreciation of one's own personhood, worth and growth is the basis for contributing without reserve to the personal growth and development of another, which is precisely what love involves. No one grows at the expense of another. While many so-called authorities in psychology and the social sciences insist that accidents of birth, unfortunate circumstances of parents, home and childhood are virtually irremediable, one's truest sense of worth comes from one's appreciation of one's humanity, which is the work of the Creator. Without a deep faith in the Fatherhood of God, whose help and direction are available to all, one can have little faith in himself or his potential. Lacking this faith one sees the very idea of loving anyone else at serious cost to oneself as ridiculous rather than as fundamental to happiness.

A genuine sense of worth never depends on one's value in the eyes of his fellow-man, a dependence on the "feeling" of being needed. Such "service" of one's fellow-man is a form of prostitution, an addiction to approval of others whose judgment is as bad or worse than one's own. This is the addiction of the climber, the power hungry, the ambitious, the performer, the exhibitionist who cannot live without the adulation, the approval of others. Many scoff at the preoccupation with God of the poor, needy and neglected. But their whole life experience has taught them that there is no reason to hope or trust in their fellow man, who is busy taking take of "Number One" at all times. For them such reliance on their fellow man as they may have had always ended in disappointment.

In our world today people are rarely given any worth simply because of their humanity, as widespread approval of both abortion and euthanasia clearly indicate. Learning to love involves a much deeper awareness of the value of man coming from what he is rather than what he does or has. There is little intrinsic worth to the man or woman in the eyes of the unloving. It is the extrinsics, such as personal or political power, riches or pleasure sources, that matter. Such short-sighted evaluations spawn the disastrous struggles among men and nations for the prestige and power to tyrannize and exploit the human brotherhood. This is the thought behind the "quality of life" pundits who would leave no stone unturned to make themselves more comfortable regardless of the costs to others. Acceptance of human life as the work of a Supreme Being is the only workable basis of the genuine respect for oneself or others involved in learning to love. Despite its widespread denial, the fact remains that one has no more or less love for another than one has for God. That God does not mean very much to many people simply indicates that other people don't matter that much to them either. Loving is so clearly the reflection of God in man, the image of God, that loving on any other basis than faith in God is a deception, a form of utilitariansim or mutual interdependence however well or thinly disguised.

Once we are convinced that loving is the meaning in life, our purpose, learning to love may well get top priority. If it does there are many ways of achieving it, all of which contribute to the end product. Loving people can teach us if we recognize them for what they are. They teach us by their lives even more than by their words, although the latter should be listened to. Because we have become accustomed to learning in school, the academic approach to loving should not be altogether excluded but seen in its limitations, and used for what it has to offer. There is so much to loving that it must be pondered, studied, as well as lived. We learn to love through experience, for which we need both insight and courage. But these are virtually worthless without humility, the love of truth so vital to the progress of every human being in the struggle with his most personal and meaningful problem, that of loving. But love can and must be both taught and learned; it must be given the priority it deserves as the most meaningful and consequential of personal achievements.

CHAPTER ELEVEN

The Personal Relationship

There are increasingly more people who for innumerable reasons remain unmarried for a long time, even for life. The refusal to be pushed or dragged into marriage through coercion, be it cultural, personal, conventional, or that of their own or others' libidos, brings these people face to face with the need for the deep, loving personal relationship. That relationship between two people exists in their very souls, occasioned perhaps by the external circumstances common in chance meetings, but developed and maintained by the need to love another human being. There are currently many alternatives to marriage for those wise enough to decline a marriage of convenience or of psuedo-necessity but who must love if they are to be fully human. Fortunately too, in the intersexual relationship there are many safeguards against irremediable consequences of honest mistakes. There is more understanding, tolerance, and even acceptance of ways of life heretofore hardly considered.

Many people choosing single life want to be good people, maintain their self-respect and integrity without being complete squares or limiting their capacity to love and be loved. They can do this if they learn to love genuinely and well. Then too, there are a number of divorced people with enough wisdom not to move from a broken marriage into a worse one, left to live single lives. Disenchanted with marriage as they have experienced it, often badly burned from the searing experience of rejection, somehow they have retained their faith in personal love and all that it involves. Many of them eventually remarry, but in the meantime they learn to love as single people: they experience life's real meaning and purpose in the personal relationship. They are not easily sucked in by the beautiful theories of permissive sex that leave so many wrecks everywhere. They may learn to love more easily because they know so well that while sex can be happy for people who love, it may not even be pleasant for those who do not, for those who use it to get what they want, whether that is a person, power or possession.

Something special must be said of the young single woman, liberated from ties to home and the sheltered life under doting parents, competing in the commercial world for attention with women who gladly let it all hang out, who insist a little too stridently that permissiveness really is the life. Single women compete on a nearly equal basis with men, who have been playing the game of grabs far longer and more ruthlessly. It is only in modern times that women have become the huge working force they are today in Western civilization (if it deserves that name). In the past, if a girl did not marry, the only alternative was to remain at home to become a domestic slave for aging parents who eventually left her behind to live out her life in loneliness. After World War I the idea of women in the labour force became acceptable, and now few women are content to go directly from school to marriage and a home. Nor are homes that easy to come by in modern urban living. Many women want to qualify themselves for a second career by spending some years single and self-supporting. They do not all want to become swingers, playing games. Still, many are desperately lonely, having escaped from the boredom of small towns to the big cities when their undoubted superiority made marriage to a local boy an unhappy prospect at best. They often find themselves particularly vulnerable and feel unequal to the effort to persist in virtue. In preference to remaining alone and lonely in the termite anonymity of high-rise urban living, they choose a temporary affair with another single person, equally unprepared for the obligations of marriage or with a married man. To these, chastity still has some meaning and offers some alternatives to sexual orgies or devastating loneliness if it leads them to discover and develop their power to love.

Loving relationships with good people are open to those willing to learn how to handle their emotions, and to learn that love is the one power that keeps the emotions from running and ruining their lives. These learn that love is not a feeling but a relationship, not mere sexuality, but a constant capable of containing and living with the sexual and other feelings, be they jealousy, resentment, anger or any of the varied emotions experienced in a real relationship with another human being. Their emotions prompt their minds to preview the tragedy of stolen hours and usurped privileges, the corniness of the pushy lovers who insist so stupidly that willing sexual co-operation is the proof of love. Wise women recognize the never-never land of unreality that is one step ahead of the abortionist's office or the home for unwed mothers. Nor are wise young men much impressed by lusty, free-living women so willing to offer "everything" for love, when "everything" is strictly of the body under pressure of their own sexual demands. History must repeat itself in the broken hearts of those who will not learn that true love is never blind, that it can clearly see what lies ahead, in or out of marriage, when there is genuine love in any relationship. Nothing so sharpens foresight as love; nothing so dulls it as lust.

Loving personal relationships are beyond people with serious emotional problems, for the very simple reason that such problems are inseparable from the preoccupation with self that militates against loving relationships. Emotional problems make it impossible for their victim to ask the objective questions clearly required to establish the basis for such relationships. People motivated completely by their own felt needs endow attractive people at a glance with the qualities they want to see in them, rather than see the characteristics that are really there. Such total subjectivity provides the poorest prospects for meaningful relationships.

The current preoccupation with the *interpersonal relationship* is man's expression of his need to love, his acknowledged failure to love. He is admitting that the dominance of the externals makes genuine friendship impossible. He senses that real love must be personal rather than sexual or homosexual; that it must be deep and lasting rather than superficially exciting but fleeting. The personal relationship is being seen more easily as the heart-to-heart friendship that transcends externals and eliminates prejudices, whether racial, religious, social, economic or whatever.

The personal relationship leaps the chasm between the attractive and the homely, the healthy and the sick, the powerful and the humble, the talented and the retarded. Certainly the personal relationship makes no distinction between the male and the female; it is wholly honest.

The obstacle to personal relationships is more and more obviously man's inability to escape externals, the things he sees, touches, tastes, etc. Despite his theoretical admission of the spiritual dimension and its admitted priority over the physical or material dimension, man continues to be dominated in 90 per cent of his thinking by externals. Just to that extent is he making personal relationships difficult. Man's soul, the faculty that guides him through life, that determines whether his hand will be raised to wound or to caress, to feed or to poison, is treated as a fiction and this despite the fact that man's actions indicate clearly the presence of the soul, the anima, the life, as surely as the illuminated bulb indicates the presence of electricity. Actually, the personal relationship is measurable by people's awareness of one another's souls, the closeness of their thoughts, ideals and goals, the degree to which they share not their wealth, their homes, money or bodies, but their lives. The difficulties in achieving personal relationships are well illustrated by the failure of most married people who share the same bed and raise families together to become even good friends, to really communicate, to share themselves with each other.

Those who are rightly described as "real" people are capable of personal relationships in which their realness is clearly visible. The real self emerges in such a relationship and manifests itself in it. The self meets the tests of real friendship, proves itself to be interested, outgoing, and loving.

Even to begin a realistic approach to a personal relationship, one must disabuse himself of the idea that to see a living human body is to see another person. On sight one knows no more about that other person than is known about a family when one looks at the house in which that family lives. Few would mistake a corpse for anything but the "remains" of a person, nor would one be deluded that a personal relationship with a corpse was possible. The personal relationship is with that dimension that has left the cadaver, that gave the body life, with the anima, the soul. It is for that reason that truly good friends are sometimes called soulmates.

The tendency in relating to others is to make the visible body the focus of attention while overlooking the invisible but more essential element of the person, the life, or the soul. The spiritual dimension of the person, which directs that person's life, is as invisible as God, for like Him, it is of an immaterial, a spiritual substance. The spiritual dimension governs the external actions of the body, the behaviour through which the person is truly known, indirectly. People see in creation the manifestation of God's presence, His work. They grasp something of His greatness by seeing what He has done. The spiritual dimension of man (the mind) programs the computer (the brain) to direct man's actions and behaviour, which reveal the person that he really is. It is because this inner person is so difficult to know that loving people can after a long association quite truthfully say, "Only now am I beginning to know you." Their long-term interest and caring has born fruit in the personal relationship, in love, personal love. People taken up with externals and superficialities never develop the interest it takes to make it to the personal relationship. They are content to think of others as desirable or undesirable according to their attractiveness or usefulness.

It shocks most people to hear that they will hardly relate better to their fellow man than they do to God, the Supreme Being, or whatever name they choose to give the source of creation. One who takes little or no notice of or interest in God, whose handiwork is all around him, will hardly have more personal interest in his neighbour. He will look on him as he looks on creation merely as a subject for exploitation, enrichment for himself. Such people are primarily interested in themselves and their own desires, likes and dislikes, and the use they can make of their fellow man. They are the number one priority in their own lives; they run their world to suit themselves and are most contented when things and people around them fit into their declared and controllable slots. These people are utterly utilitarian and unloving.

A relationship with God begun early in life is the greatest asset in directing one's attention away from oneself, which is the fundamental requirement for loving. Those absorbed in themselves do not relate to others. They develop into self-centred, neurotic exploiters. The calamity of self-orientation starts very early. The newborn child quickly reaches for the things that attract it, and soon for people. When his reception is encouraged, his interest and ability in relating develop, flourish. Meeting unpleasant or hostile reaction he withdraws, and his outreach withers. Then, only the influence of many and good loving people can neutralize or compensate for the penalty of such experience. The availability of such people underlies the story of every loving man or woman and the development of the personal relationship. Nothing so helps the young moving into personal relationships as having lived in a home where they saw firsthand good, healthy family relationships. Those who acquire wisdom and make good practical judgments easily have generally had such a loving childhood and youth.

The onset of puberty and the pressure of the mating instinct really test the power of love to surmount the gravitational pull to what is desired rather than to what is good for oneself and others. Yet few people who relate well personally before the age of puberty are thrown off by the sexual maturing process. The pressure of sexual desires simply cannot rob them of awareness of others and their genuine good. To be conceived in lust and born into an atmosphere of selfishness and narcissism is as poor a preparation for the personal relationship as growing up under parental indifference or neglect. Here again, whatever hope there may be for the child will come with the advent into his life of truly loving people who open the way for him to the personal relationship.

Loving people are thoroughly concern-invested in those they love. Their love is simply not dominated by their own pleasure or comfort, nor is it possessive or exclusive; It is willful, expansive and inclusive. The loving person finds room in his life for all. His interest in each one is genuine because of his genuine interest in all. He can share himself with anyone and does so with all but within the human limitations that exclude both the ego trip and blatant disregard for the real priorities to be respected in his own private, personal life. His easy relations with people originate not in blindness to the weakness of people but rather in his faith in the human potential of each. He really believes in people. His love is very human and personal, never angelic nor unreal, but of body and soul. His love is always good for the loved ones, whom he never exploits for his own or anyone else's emotional satisfaction. The life of such a person is characterized by loving personal relationships, which are proliferated through his associations and by his associates, enriched as they are by their experience of him.

Those able to enrich the lives of others through personal loving never give things priority over people. They simply do not have that personal void in their lives which unloving people feel compelled to fill with things. The latter are the people whose lives are dominated by social prestige, political power, palatial residences, liquor and other drugs, pleasure, money, food, and the myriad other luxuries and status symbols.

The use of people as sex objects is incompatible with the personal relationship, and so is the use of things as bribes to get what one wants or to stimulate children or friends to achieve for one's own honour and glory. The one whose life is characterized by personal relationships values money, material possessions and personal comforts only as things to be shared gratefully, used without fear of loss, without coveting the security they so falsely represent to the undiscerning. The use of things can only be regulated happily by love, by people-oriented people.

In our society external appearances have too great a role in opening or closing the way to personal relationships. It is so human to be attracted by the attractive, repelled by the repulsive. Yet experience in personal relationships makes one wary of such reactions. Delusion is the lot of those too quick to attribute personal attractiveness to the attractive body, or personal repulsiveness to the repulsive body. The former too often belong to the proud, arrogant, self-indulgent and spoiled, while within the latter may be discovered truly beautiful people. Those capable of personal relationships are not so easily deceived. Their emphasis has long been on the inner person, where true beauty dwells. They have the happy faculty of divining the rich vein of ore deep under the surface, well hidden in the extraordinary human potential.

The key to personal relationships is locked into the Christian obligation, which even the best of Christians struggle with somewhat disbelievingly, the duty to love one's enemies. This struggle has produced varied versions and explanations of the differences between liking and loving, between goodwill and affection. The most common explanation is that people have a native inability to like repulsive people, the ill-behaved, the moral or physical leper, the deformed, retarded or physically handicapped, the criminal, alcoholic or grossly ugly. Those who accept this idea are unaware that the loving person's vision is not restricted to what he sees with the eye, for he has depth perception that reveals the person underneath the revolting spectacle. Only those not deceived by externals can relate to the real person in the deformed or criminal body. They see with faith that every human being, regardless of present state or apppearance, possesses the beauty inherent in the human potential. That inherent richness needs only development to become apparent to the genuinely interested. The interest of one capable of relating personally brings out the first suspicion in many heretofore ugly people that they have a hidden beauty that sets them apart. Most unattractive people, rejected by the superficial and discriminated against by the selfish, are so fear-dominated in their personal relationships that they have no clue to their inner beauty. How then can they reveal it to anyone? Those who see persons when they look at people know all too well how tremendous is the loss in human resources to our world because of the personal failure to relate.

Even the selfish marvel at the obvious joy of those dedicating their lives to the underprivileged. There seems so little emotional reward or feedback from such work, such unreal selflessness. But those who value the human person, however disguised, do get a feedback much more meaningful than an emotional one. There are indeed people who work for the less fortunate because they can always feel superior. However, such people are neither dedicated nor loving. They neither help the unfortunate nor do they grow themselves; rather, they tyrannize their charges and frustrate themselves. The feedback to the truly dedicated lies in their awareness of the growth and self-reliance of their charges, the emergence of personality in the deep sense of that word, true humanness.

The strong underlying motivation in euthanasia of the unfit is the acute discomfort of the unloving in the presence of the outwardly ugly. They see no more than their eyes reveal. Evaluation based on externals is generally low, for the simple reason that such an assessment denies the existence let alone the value of the internal dimension—the soul. This explains the general lionizing of physically, socially, financially attractive people despite their inner ugliness, quite apparent to loving people. The humanity of the deformed is not missing, merely impeded; the inwardly ugly are so much more lacking in true humanity. Most of the physically or mentally retarded do enjoy their lives, regardless of their limitations and inescapable pain. It takes very little loving care to increase their enjoyment. Yet many people give much greater care to their animals. They would probably be arrested if they did not. The care of the retarded does so much for those who provide it. It assures that they live truly, personally, liberating their love from dependence on the emotional feedback to which so many are slaves and which puts true personal relationships beyond reach.

Possibly the inability to read the emotions correctly is the greatest obstacle to personal relationships. Certainly anyone who identifies love with "falling in love" because of the similarity of feelings originating in novelty, the thrilling discovery of mutual interests and understanding (always accompanied with sensual and pleasurable emotions), will never make it to genuine personal relationships. However close to the venereal such emotions may be, there is a great difference. Love is between persons who are sexual by nature, who relate well personally and are made aware of it by their feelings, but the relationship is neither sexual, nor emotionally dominated, but personal. It is by completely misreading these emotions that the direction of the relationship may become genital. The problem of homosexuality illustrates this very well. Two people of the same sex may be quite normally and naturally drawn to each other. When these two people are sexually dominated, self-indulgent, they will quite readily mistake the pleasurable emotions of discovery and openness to each other—personal intimacy—for a sexual one. Then, instead of developing the personal relationship, force of habit leads them right into the sexual one. This exploitation spells the end of the relationship, however determined they may be to keep it going.

The case of the genuine celibate commitment also illustrates this problem, as does the respected marital commitment. In both these cases, although the emotions involved in a new-found, exciting friendship might easily be misunderstood to the extent of subsequent misdirection of the relationship, when people are definitely committed to a course that eliminates the genital they tend to direct their relationship into the personal. And the personal relationship does survive the challenge of the emotions to be misunderstood. The sexual is not avoided, but surpassed or surmounted. Of course, any person who makes and keeps a committment is indeed mature. Maturity is the stuff of a the lasting personal relationship.

The problem of the homosexual is the same as that of the heterosexual. Sex is simply overemphasized as a means of relating personally. After all if physical proximity necessarily brought people closer personally, one would be closer to the next person in the rush-hour subway than to most of one's own family. Unforunate experience and poor guidance from misunderstanding of human sexuality compel deeper attention to an interest in personal relationships. Personal growth and the deepening of relationships do not lie in the physical, pleasurable, sexual dimension but in the willful personal achievement of genuine love. Sexuality is never better handled than in the good personal relationships. Problems, if not absent, are minimal. The homosexual problem is that sex has been allowed and encouraged to take on an importance that it simply does not and cannot have. The good personal relationship finds sex in its rightful place, neither repressed nor exploited, lived within its rightful limits, with its rightful importance no more, no less.

Genuine interest in another must, sooner or later, strike the spark of goodness in the loved one, exploding it into the delight of personal fulfilment. Seeing this happen a few times is enough to make one concede the primacy of the personal relationship, that this is the way love works and the very reason it is so desired and sought after. Everyone experiences that it is not good for man to be alone. True love provides the delight of sharing. However, any delight grabbed greedily threatens the personal relationship. The exploited personal relationship proves to have been planted in very shallow earth.

Because the dimensions of the inner person are spiritual, all but limitless, the personal relationship survives familiarity, boredom, disappointment and time. It provides a security independent of transient feelings or superficial qualities, a security based on personal interest through which it is begun, develops and endures.

So unique, rewarding and fulfilling is the genuinely deep, loving, personal relationship that most people want desperately to believe they have such a relationship when any objective observer could easily disabuse them of such a notion. Innumerable young people claim it for themselves on mere acquaintance or infatuation, when such a relationship obviously can only be the fruit of years of loving experience and growth. So great are such friendships that most people could live a lifetime on one or two of them. Anyone who claims many for himself must be joking. The emotional stability they provide is the basis of very meaningful, long-term living in human relationships. A healthy community depends on them, be that community a family, a religious or social commune, a village, a city or a nation.

People who manifest discomfort in the presence of the opposite sex are "paper tigers" whose humanity and inner strength has never developed. They are not persons enough to sustain the personal relationship; they lack the personal identity and sense of worth it takes for such relationships. For some reason, perhaps unhappy experience, being alone with one of the opposite sex seems an insuperable obstacle to virtue rather than the very occasion of it. For such people, who expect physical fitness to come from exercise, seem to expect inner, spiritual, moral strength to come by magic or some miraculous infusion of grace rather than from the actual graces of contending with daily associations, the occasions of virtue. Male or female chauvinism is a natural pitfall for such people, a ready excuse for avoiding personal relationships.

Chauvinism is the basic defense line of the threatened and insecure and thus of the unemerged, underdeveloped person. Therefore the chauvinist, male or female is a poor candidate for true personal relationships. The chauvinist has too little faith in his or her true worth and therefore has to resort to some technical defence, explanation, or rationalization. For every charge of male chauvinism there is quite logically a countercharge of female chauvinism, with little choice between the evils. The much greater similarities between male and female consist in their personhood; the differences lie in their maleness and femaleness. The love that makes them friends provides their personal equality and so true relationship. True love never speaks as anything but personal equal to personal equal however disproportionate their talents and achievements. The love that endows equality, eliminates or at least diminishes prejudice, bigotry, snobbery, exploitation and the myriad vices of human society. The personal relationship disarms the chauvinist. There is neither talking down to nor up to in the personal relationship, because real interest or love can be no more obsequious than patronizing. The genuine personal relationship can never magically produce an equality of age, wisdom, station, spiritual or material endowment, but it does produce a personal equality. To the degree that an accusing finger can rightly point to a male-dominated world, it is pointing to an unloving world. Nor will it be more loving if and when it is female-dominated. A world that represents only power and force is incapable of love. But people who reach true personhood in loving can eliminate chauvinism in relationships that are truly personal.

While the personal relationship confers equality, it never demands it. Nor does it confuse equality with identity. It does recognize and respect superiority when it meets it. Women have wrongfully been considered the weaker sex despite overwhelming evidence, in many areas of living, of a strength far surpassing that of most men. Only the undoubted superiority of many women as persons enabled them to achieve their goals despite oppression. For generations, by guile, wile and smile they have unzipped male egos for innumerable worthy and unworthy purposes. Women in their rightful places, speaking as unquestioned equals, however different they may be in design, potential and role, exercise extraordinary influence. Many are undoubtedly superior persons because culturally, they have been freer to love than have men. As superior people they have had greater access to truly personal relationships. Men have tended to marry the women they want, while women have tended to learn to love the men they married. They had to be superior to do that. Through their loving they became real persons. Such loving women historically have been the main source of strength, inspiration and support of almost all great men. They return gift or outcome of such unions was a security so personal as to be indestructible. Surely wise women realize how much is to be lost in the feigned equality of the sick permissive world confusing equal wrongs for equal rights. Women are never improved by becoming as bad as men. The crying need for male and female alike is the strong, loving, personal relationship characteristic of the mature adult human being. A personal relationship is made of all the strength of which one is capable, depending on all the strength another provides. It is rich; it is lasting.

People terribly engrossed in the material have so little spiritual awareness that they are poor candidates for personal relationships.

The loveless life produces cantankerous, small-minded people, prone to bickering jealousy, constantly resentful of the friendships of others—an indictment of their own unloving. Such unhappiness can to some degree be attributed to an already mentioned badly directed approach to God. Inadequate spiritual advisers, projecting their own jealousy and exclusive possessiveness of holiness, were much too concerned with avoiding bad relationships to have time to develop good ones. Few recognized in their constant suspicions of others in loving situations the projection of their own natural but suppressed sexual desires. When not exposed for what they are such suspicions, already negative and cruel, easily become sadistic. These are the people to whom the lurid episodes reported in the sensationalist press appeal greatly, though they would never be caught reading them; the fearful relish vicariously the secretly envied exploits of others. The market for such commercial enterprises indicates clearly the number of loveless lives. Such people are prone to nervous breakdowns; they are the perfectionists so wrongly sure that the approval they need so badly depends on their performance rather than on their value as human beings. These are the people who give gifts solely to indebt the beneficiaries to themselves forever. These are the ones so fearful of rejection because of their feelings of worthlessness, those who could not possibly accept that someone else sees a worth in them of which they themselves are not aware. The loveless, wise enough to sense at last that no one need have a nervous breakdown, to understand, sooner or later, that no one is making the ridiculous demands of them that they make of themselves, to eventually see emotional ill health as evidence of a terribly wrong set of values, have help available if they want it. They can be healed if they are humble enough to turn to someone who loves them, and ask for help, for truth, for understanding and support. Since one who loves will never exploit their temporary dependence but is anxious to see them made whole, real love is the cure they need. The pain they experience in learning to relate is worth all the anguish in it. The personal relationship is born in pain in the risk of the anguish of rejection.

Educated but unloving man is truly retarded, unbalanced and defenceless. For so long man has told himself that if he were educated his future would be assured, only to learn now how hopeless he is without love, loving. Until now the academic diploma has been the passport to self realization and affluence, granted for the faithful worship of material progress. If and when the reign of academe is re-evaluated, if heart as well as head is put into academic education, if people and relationships between them are given high priority, man may yet be as good as he is smart. The reign of love could then begin. Then man will be more important than his money, or possessions. He will then have reason to live.

When a good man speaks of a good relationship with a good woman, his words are generally received with either disbelief or morbid fear of scandal. It is as if God's commandment to love should be taken with a grain of salt because He is asking more of man than he can do. There is a cultural inheritance of historic mistakes and exploitation in intersexual relationships but this is not because of love but because of pride and arrogance, the very qualities in a person that are eliminated by a well-developed power to love. The morbid fear of wrongdoing, and more often, of being caught, dominates the lives of fearful people, so much more capable of shame for sin than of sorrow for it. Such people do not grasp the essential role of love in the development and growth of man, to say nothing of the awful scandal of unloving. Surely their fears are more inspired by the weakness of their sinners than the greatness of their saints. It is such fears that have created the historic portrait of the pious churchman shunning the finest woman as an occasion of sin while carrying around in his purse the fruit of his greed, remaining all the while convinced of his qualification to direct the world to God.

The combination of the power to love with the grace of God is what the theologians reject when they insist that personal relationships are inevitably sex-dominated. They quote their home-made rules, which they use both to excuse their own weakness and to justify their fears, to dispense themselves from the painful development of their own potentials. They write off both the grace of God and the potential of man when they reckon the dangers in loving as unmanageable and the occasions of loving as occasions of sin. The world surely has little incentive to believe in a love which even the theologians discount because they do not have the virtue to practice it.

Whoever refuses to be sex-dominated either negatively through fear of it or positively through passion finds that relationships based on the real good of others lead to depths of friendship hitherto unsuspected. Loving deeply, such a person finds himself or herself a man or a woman in the very best sense of the word. Such love is not as far above the ordinary person as many would make it. Recorded history preferred intrigue to the honest account of thousands who like Thomas Moore, so loved people and a truthful cause that even their vital needs and life itself was transcended. If love is really harder than that, people should forget it, for then God would surely have set a goal beyond achievement. Scientists and artists, so engrossed in their work that sex is forgotten or ignored, show clearly the power of the mind and will to direct life purposefully despite the strongest emotions.

An irreversible commitment to love as the human goal opens the way to learning a great deal. As one lives through his first experience of deep personal love, he clearly sees that neither sex nor marriage is essential to love, but are both limited experiences of their own. He grasps that he can love several people uniquely and well, and that none of these people displaces another. When love is genuine, each one loved develops a deep, personal respect for the others and all are brought closer to lover and loved one. Furthermore, the more genuinely loving one is, the more likely that his love will be cross-cultural, cross-racial and supranational. He lives a brotherhood instinctively sensed by those with whom he lives and works. He is immune to the ego trip of the social messiah or the naiveté of the do-gooder. He simply cannot be trapped by the deceptions involved in a white man hating a black while assuming incorrectly that he loves other whites, his own, and vice versa. Or again, an anti-Semite being deluded that he loves anyone. The great hater works so hard at unloving that he robs life of its meaning, the personal relationships of people fully alive.

CHAPTER TWELVE

Premarital Love.

Premarital relationships offer a special challenge to come to grips with love as the directing force of one's life. Premarital love is a time of intensive one to one relating, with the full pressure of the sexual polarity and the incentive inherent in the expectation of many years of close living. There is a great reason for trying to make the premarital association a time of true love on a very personal basis. However, there are many problems inevitable in this situation. Premarital loving is nearly impossible when loving has not begun well before courtship. Again, there is nothing about the premarital association which makes one loving although it may occasion love. Finally, if genuine love in a truly personal relationship does not at least begin in premarital association it becomes harder and harder to love in married life.

Several serious misconceptions about marriage must be clarified if premarital love is ever to become a reality. Centuries of socalled romantic love have led to broad acceptance of the totally false notion that there is something essentially loving about marriage. There is not. A marriage is loving only if and when the people in it are loving. In most of the world marriage never had and still has not any direct relationship to love. It is a social admission to adulthood and a time to arrange sexual living related to the family unit and its role in the prevailing culture and society. So there is no sudden blossoming in courtship of a genuine personal love which has not existed prior to courtship.

In Western culture people generally go most willingly into the marriage from which they expect to get the most material benefit. They marry someone they want rather than someone they love. It is not that they should marry someone they do not want but merely that love is not getting what one wants but giving what one has. Love is obviously the ability and willingness to live for others, to identify and equate the good of others with one's own good, to put others on a par with oneself. One does have some control over what one gives in marriage but very little over what one is to receive. That depends on the ability and willingness of one's partner to love. Love is assured in marriage only to the degree that one gives oneself. In today's permissive society marriage is looked upon as unacceptably restrictive precisely because its demands are so great and its obvious benefits so few. It offers great opportunity to give but little guarantee of receiving. Since relatively few people in marriage are genuinely loving most look for what they expect from marriage to explain its importance. The current divorce rate indicates a general disenchantment with marriage. The unwillingness to pay the high cost of loving is clearly seen in the rebellion against the high financial and emotional cost of divorce. This leaves premarital love as about the only available insurance against divorce and broken homes, the spawning grounds of emotional cripples.

Marriage must be seen today for what it generally is rather than for what people romantically expect or hope it to be. It is not generally the climax of a loving, man to woman, personal relationship but it is generally the end result of the mating and nesting instincts which people do share with the birds and the bees. The sexual polarity (shared with animals) does draw young people together, who then "fall in love", a highly exciting emotional experience of very little personal significance, and then, imagine they have achieved sufficient relationship to unite for life. So wrong is this concept that little but tragedy can ensue. These young people had barely begun to grapple with the reality that love is. Marriage then with all its cultural, though false, promise of happiness is much too difficult an assignment for most young people to handle well under today's conditions. It is becoming more and more obvious that only premarital love makes it possible to hope realistically for a happy marriage, the normal source of loving homes and children.

To this end then, young people have got to understand sex for all that it really is and everything that it really is not. They have to be immune to the pressure of sex as an incentive to marriage. They must never be pushed as they often are by over-anxious parents, or modern society's mores, into precipitous marriages for which they are not prepared. For society to make divorce easy, provide it at little or no financial or emotional cost, is the poorest answer to this problem. The real one is do everything in one's power to make clear the difference between sex and love, to teach people to handle their sexual and other emotions well as the indispensable condition to loving well, and to teach young people to gladly defer the age of marriage until a time when they have begun to be loving people. It is simply horrendous, and totally irresponsible, to teach sex in such a way as to make it seem a natural thing to which everyone has a right even at an age when other matters of equal importance in life are clearly seen to be beyond the understanding and management of the obviously immature. It is most ridiculous to throw young people into tremendously compelling emotional relationships long before they have reached even emotional, let alone personal maturity without expecting the tragic results everywhere apparent today, in drug addiction, broken homes, troubled people, neglected and undisciplined children.

Sex education whether in the home or in the school, by parents or teachers, highly trained social scientists, psychologists or psychiatrists has to be a disaster unless it is made plain from the beginning that human sex is tied essentially and inescapably into the central human power to love, and that out of this context it not only makes no sense but can lead to nothing more or less than personal tragedy for the individual and/or society, and that, regardless of all the pains and costs society takes to obviate the end results of premature sexual activity or promiscuity. It is simply impossible to teach or even imply the possibility of easily accessible sexual indulgence without heavy responsibility and yet hope that love might possibily be even the accidental consequence of such action. After all, love is the most responsible and meaningful human action or state, and it is totally antithetic to the self-oriented exploitation encouraged in a smug technological society presumptuously ignoring that which makes sex human, its role in loving.

Valid sex education must make it clear that the genitals are not toys to be played with, not merely things that people have, but which are accompanied with very great desires that vary not merely with time, age, opportunity, incitement and other factors, but which must for happiness be dominated by the power to love. Valid sex should point out very clearly and forcefully that underlying the sexual expression is the very real human desire not merely to get into the body of another person but to get in to the life of that person, lovingly, not merely to take another person into one's own body but to take that other person lovingly into one's life. When this awareness is not only real but the governing factor in sex, then that sex is truly human rather than merely animal. In other words in humanity no act can be merely sexual and be meaningful. To be meaningful it has to be dominantly personal, lovingly personal, truly human.

Sex education should make it clear to young people just what it is that makes them desire to disrobe for each other, to see each other in naked intimacy, to see each other as "they really are." Even a child can learn, as they do in primitive societies and cultures, that physical nakedness is no great thing. After all there are only two variations of human structure. The real intimacy that people want and need to share is the intimate nakedness of self-revelation, personal insight, being seen and accepted for what they really are as people in the security afforded by genuine love, a love in which nothing can separate them. Love is the beginning of this intimacy which continues its growth with the passing years of deepening confidence and trust. This is the only intimacy which can defy boredom because it continues indefinitely to reveal new horizons and personal dimensions, things sex simply cannot provide. When oblivious of the depths and meaning of personal intimacy people easily become sexual faddists desperately divising new ways and means of exploring the very shallow physical limits of the human body.

The physical relationship cannot survive boredom; the personal one can and does. Sexual exploration has so little to offer in comparison to the rich yield from exploration of the depths of the human person. Premarital love consists in the ability to grasp this principle, to relate well on a personal, one to one basis.

Sex education to be realistic let alone effective, should be aimed at the attainment of premarital love, at the role of loving as expressed in and through the sexual dimensions. Certainly sex educators should be very much aware of the serious problem involved in showing how much more there is to loving than sex. The main thesis in sex education ought to be that the loving person handles his or her sexual life very much in the same way he or she handles all other relationships and vital experiences, that is, lovingly. Can one expect a power-hungry, money-greedy, exploitative business-man to leave these qualities at his job and suddenly become a tender, loving, considerate person in his sexual life at home? As a matter of fact, it is only when the sex education program is an extension of the emphasis on kindness, goodness, thoughtfulness and loving that it contributes to the achievement of a wholesome sexual life. Any child well trained in these virtues absorbs sex education without detriment. Sex education without this training has proven everywhere a disappointment, its effectiveness limited to minimizing the ravages of sex abuse. Sex education is a misnomer for the revelation of sex secrets as an ever-ready source of unrestrained pleasure, as compensation for every disappointment in life. The object of sex education is achieved when young people reach the time of courtship so understanding sex and its role in human relationships that they accept the real limitations of sex as an expression of personal love. They would then be less apt to divorce sex from the power to love which gives it meaning.

Sex education in preparation for premarital love must come up with more than right answers. It must include the motivation and strength to put those answers into practical living. Love is the only effective motivation and virtue the only practical strength. Sexual maturation in the human sense involves much more than physical ability. It involves the ability to live responsibly at cruising speed with the sexual emotions, something quite impossible for the victims of permissive training. Permissiveness begun and encouraged long before the sexual, prepuberty impulses are experienced vitiates the best of sex instruction. People who would not bake a cake without a recipe strangely expect to make sense of their lives with neither direction nor discipline.

Proper sex instruction combined with wisdom and strength saves innumerable loving relationships outside marriage, avoids tragic mistakes and needless hurt to many innocent people involved in the breakups of homes and families. The combination of knowledge and virtue clearly indicates the sexual glands as mechanically responsive to feelings of tenderness, flashing early warning, channeling the anxiety they create into responsible concern rather than compulsion to copulate in a meaningless way. Premarital love sees the sexual emotions as blind faculites responding automatically to physical stimuli unless deliberately inhibited. Though differing in intensity and degree from a full genital reaction, personal tenderness evokes a sexual response which proper understanding and judgment enable one to accept without qualm or concern. Precisely through such understanding the inhibiting mechanisms available to mind and will are directed to thoughtful loving.

Those who reject any inhibition as destructive overlook the widespread use of these mechanisms in public relations, the achieving of a good image. One easily learns to react inwardly without lashing out and revealing himself. One reacts hungrily without snatching food from others, or bolting it ravenously. One feels the need of a drink without getting drunk. Surely such mechanisms could hardly serve a better purpose than preserving premarital love from destruction by sexual pleasure exploitation. It does take strength to use such mechanisms to direct a lover's attention to the loved one rather than allow sexual excitement to carry the day. The use of these mechanisms does depend on genital excitation being recognized for what it is, a normal fact of emotional life, utterly without moral overtones and indispensable in directing one's attention to the loved one.

Premarital love is not easy. Sexual maturity comes so much earlier than personal maturity. Society, the media, the rejection of old taboos and cultural hangups all push the young towards premature sexual experience long before they are capable of genuine personal value judgments. Too many insist that one can wait for love whereas it is too hard to wait for sex. Yet the opposite is true. Sex can wait but love must not. The earlier the beginning of love the better one handles the sexual life, while on the other hand the earlier the sexual indulgence the more difficult genuine loving becomes. Youthful emphasis on self does not dispose to loving awareness of others. Confusion from this self-other dichotomy gives support to the argument for trial marriage. The obvious devastation originating in hasty marriages under the pressure of sexual compulsion leads too easily to the argument that young people should first live together to find love through sexual compatibility. The sexual and loving lives are not so easily separated, but true sexual compatibility comes through love. Sexual compatibility in itself more often than not simply indicates two people with equal disregard for the essential meaning and role of genital sex. Trial marriage's essential purpose is to use and be used, to avoid personal harm or serious inconvenience, a purpose diametrically opposed to the selfdisciplined respect and solicitous care for others which is love.

Trial marriage would be better called trial sex, the arrangement between two people for a full genital life outside a commitment to a lasting marriage. This is hardly more than a form of "free love" better called free sex. It only takes time to discover the actual costs of free sex. The payment is not in cash but it is always very expensive. A standard truism says that anyone who marries another for money earns every cent of it. Trial marriage could well be called a "pay as you play" game. Centuries of effort have produced not a single way to have one's cake and eat it too, to have the privileges without the obligations. The mutually willing provision of bodies for selfgratification is quite incompatible with love even in marriage. Premarital love is the unmarried, personal, loving relationship with the sexual emotions neither exploited nor suppressed but lived with maturely and responsibly. This situation is completely at odds with trial marriage.

Personal integrity reserves the genital function to husbands and wives, mothers and fathers, those making a permanent, personal commitment to each other in marriage, an exclusive, genital sexual availability to each other quite incompatible with irresponsible sex. The statistics of those who have tried it otherwise are overwhelming and conclusive. Can one honestly believe he loves deeply while using contraceptives with someone to whom he is unwilling or unable to make a legal, lifetime commitment? To insist that it is the actual rather than the legal commitment which is important is a farce. The "free" marriage in which each party lives his own life on his own terms is "no" marriage, but the mirage created by rationalizing, double-talk, con-artists. When sex is all they want they should hardly be surprised that it is all they get. It is no bargain on their terms when it is actually available everywhere on even easier terms. The use of the genitals as a valid expression of love does not have to protect itself against that expression.

Sex never takes the dominant role however strongly felt between friends, however close, who intend to stay single. The genital function used outside of marriage deprives a relationship of the security and respect inherent in the personal commitment basic to true love. Courting lovers know this. The multitudes who disagree with this statement have already decided what they want to be true regardless of any and all experience to the contrary. Because they have chosen to identify sex with love they reject the concept that love does make sexual intercourse superfluous in any circumstance which would reasonably exclude sex, where actual needs ought to exclude felt desires.

Premarital love is made more difficult by the tendency of young people to marry too young, to marry the one they want, to be selective rather than loving in their relationships. Selectivity is based on desire and opportunity to get what one wants. Marriage ought to be the opportunity to give and share what one has. Marriage, especially early marriage presents very little likelihood of getting what one wants for that depends entirely on the other person's loving generosity. The discerning person, and that ought to exclude anyone dominated by the desire for what one wants, even the desire for love, ought to dismiss as a partner in marriage any emotionally dominated person. For these people find it nearly impossible to give or to share. Poor risks in personal relationships, such people are even worse risks in marriage. The basic concept that it is much more important to love than to be loved totally escapes them. Premarital love is well within the grasp of anyone setting out to see that he or she becomes a loving person.

The tendency of our times and culture to throw people headlong into premature sexual encounters is far from the greatest obstacle to premarital love, but it is a critical one. The management of such encounters well or even minimizing the consequences of them requires good solid virtue. Wisdom and strength, perhaps better called judgment and discipline are indispensable to success in anything from Art to Zen. They are basic to love. The ability to love is no accident. It is the end result of knowledge, understanding, motivation, judgment, efficacious experience, but above all, of hard work. Genuine wisdom clearly sees love as the meaning and purpose of life, and concedes to it undisputed priority in life. Added to this wisdom is the ability and facility in foregoing any and every exploitation of others, personal or sexual, as love requires. The virtue, power or strength by which sexual encounters are best handled, by which addiction to sexual pleasure is avoided, by which the tendency to look on others as sexual objects is eradicated, is precisely the virtue of chastity.

The fundamental difficulty in loving sexually is that genital sex has such a high incoming pleasure content, much too easily sought as an end in itself. The pleasure is so high that in it, one easily loses awareness of the other person which genuine personal love makes impossible. Sex is loving when in the full force of the incoming pleasure the primary focus of one's attention continues to be the other person's total welfare. Only great strength makes that possible and that strength is the virtue of chastity, something as impressive as it is rare.

It can be stated categorically that there can be no personal love without chastity. It must never be mistaken for prissy, naive, puritanical Victorianism. Chastity is not to be identified with the sexlessness so often artfully achieved by sexual repression in professional celibates, in order to deal easily with a difficult obligation. This horrendous mistake littered the path to love of the emotionally crippled with frustration and grief. Sexlessness, however achieved, provides lonely bitterness as the only viable alternative to unchastity. It writes off as impossible the chastity fundamental to the loving personal relationship for which man was given the gift of life. Chastity is totally incompatible with the generally promoted ignorance of sex, for generations fostered for the protection of the innocent. This ignorance was closely related to the suppression of the imagination, also erroneously identified with chastity. The loss to the loving person of the imagination was incalculable, on a par with making sex an inescapable source of insurmountable temptation rather than the very material of chastity. To all these and many other mistaken notions of chastity can be attributed the general deprivation of countless good people of the very input required for their emotional and even mental health. More will be said of the role of the imagination in chastity and loving, but now suffice it to say that the misguided suppression of the imagination led to the sublimation of the sexual dimension into conformity to the system, to domination by the need for approval of any authority however wrong or even evil, to acceptance of the conventions of a selfrighteous and unloving society. Such suppression is the mark of those following rigid sexual prohibitions while losing themselves in unrestrained love for money, power and luxury of all sorts. Finally, the withdrawn inability to relate to others which characterizes emotional illness should never be mistaken for chastity.

Chastity is the virtue which places the genital function completely at the disposal of the loving person to be used or left unused as love requires. It flows from the wisdom and strength to direct the sexual dimension to the deepening of the personal relationship. A society or person which rejects it simply cannot be a loving one.

Chastity is to personal love what budgeting is to finance. When money means too much or too little it dominates and wrecks one's life. One must know when to spend and when to reserve, when to risk and when to be cautious, when to invest or dispose of capital, when something is within or beyond one's reach, when to indulge or curb the desire to exchange money for other things, but fundamentally when right use of money makes life meaningful and when wrong use of it vitiates life. Chastity differentiates between one's sexual wants and needs, guides one through the shoals of seduction by what is within reach or frustration by what is out of reach. That is precisely how chastity assures the right relationship of sex to love.

Confrontation with the sexual dimension is the very milieu of chastity. There can hardly be a worse milieu than the sexual segregation so widespread in the celibate dominated training of young people. The implication of such segregation is that sex is larger than people. It addresses itself primarily to the weakness of people rather than the power of God. Sexual segregation sets minimal limits to virtue and accepts the immaturity of the "good" as normal. Real and enduring love is out of the reach of those people who cannot be chaste in the normal course of human relationships, whose chastity is so meagre as to make it impossible for them to live with the genital reality. Certainly if those promoting sexual segregation have any basis in fact for their theories then they have done more to promote homosexuality than to challenge people to the indispensable virtue of chastity. Chastity is the power which in intimate associations with attractive people of the opposite sex (or the same sex) directs one's sexual actions to the real good of the one loved. Thus, regardless of sexual feelings, pleasure needs or wants, one is strong enough to do what the good of the other requires. Chastity is the fruit of genuine values, depth understanding and discipline. It is learned in the milieu of sexual integration from childhood when respect for others is acquired.

Chastity is acquired by people who live their sexual lives the best way rather than the theologically imposed "safest way". In playing sexual situations the "safe" way one gives top priority to oneself. Love demands equal priority for others. "Safe way" theology is that of the man who buried his talent, quite unChristian. How does one acquire chastity by avoiding every occasion for its practice? Permissive society has taken a terrible toll of such people totally unprepared as they were for life in permissive society, its inescapable tests and trials. "Safe way" theology deprives otherwise normal men and women of the awareness that to be male or female they must live with the normal human sexual desires and impulses, and that contending with these is the occasion of personal strength. "Safe way" theology left young people preparing for marriage ready to capitulate to the sexual pressures of courting as quite beyond their strength. It also explains the general admission of lust to the Christian marriage bed where so few negotiate the sexual relationship to the personal one on which the happiness of marriage depends. Lust has proven just as destructive in marriage as before marriage.

Young married people are not as mature as they will be later when they have grown in loving. However, premarital associations are part of the maturing process if arbitrary limits are not set to the personal strengths of the young. Such limits set by fearful, overprotective parents and religious teachers, as well as the externally imposed discipline so destructive of integrity have to be rejected in favour of selfdiscipline and awareness of the inviolability of the integrity of others, which love assures. Surely if one rejects the former without having achieved the latter only disaster can ensue. Only the fine line of a true conscience separates liberation from irresponsibility. Chastity cannot co-exist with the general torpor of selfindulgent people. To esteem and acquire chastity one must have considerable respect for the inner personal strength which is virtue.

Everyone reacts emotionally, that is identifies a new experience with an old one and immediately reacts not to what is happening but to what has happened in the past. Virtue is the inner power which contains such reactions to allow the mind to be applied to appraisal of the new situation for what it really is, and to act accordingly rather than merely react. Chastity then is the virtue which contains sexual reactions either of attraction or aversion enabling one to address oneself to the person met. One then neither pursues the attractive nor dismisses the unattractive person but begins to relate personally, addressing oneself to the personal rather than the sexual encounter, thus, neither falling madly in love with the attractive person nor dismissing the unattractive person as a "dog". Such chastity leads to personal relations in which the love of the person depends neither on attractiveness nor any other obviously impressive qualities, but on what that person actually is, the human potential for greatness and goodness which is really there. So chastity is a virtue which enables youth to avoid the hot and cold running relationships which are generally superficial and meaningless. It makes it as unthinkable to misuse another's body as to steal his money.

Chastity is virtually impossible without a clear understanding and acceptance of the genital reality. This understanding makes it clear that in courtship, when sexual excitement compels sexual exploitation, this exploitation is the general pattern of the relationship. Not only will this exploitation not cease in marriage but will be experienced on a much broader scale than the sexual. Sexual exploitation in courtship merely exposes the personal qualities which later on destroy marriage relationships. It puts beyond reach the level of personal acceptance required for good and dear friends to live together with sufficient trust to assure security. Proponents of trial marriage or open marriage merely deny that such a degree of security really exists. It is an indictment of sexual mismanagement in courtship that loving marriages are so few as to make this denial seem reasonable.

Puritanism makes premarital sex a taboo rather than a fairly normal experience with enough unhappy side effects to often neutralize it as a learning experience. While sexual experience makes little contribution towards a loving person, neither does a sterile, physical virginity. There are many worse problems than premarital sex. Every human experience has some quotient of learning in it, however unfortunate it may be. Certainly the non-virgin who is understanding, human and mature will love better than the subhuman, emotionally crippled, selfcentred, fearful virgin. The physical fact of virginity has often been more important than the virtue of virginity. Chastity is no more to be identified with inexperience, immaturity, ignorance and fear than sexual experience is to be identified with wisdom, understanding, maturity and sophistication. It is loving virginity directly related to personal integrity providing a near immunity to the exploitation of self and others which is meaningful. This flows from the kind of respect for oneself that makes it relatively easy to appreciate the inherent worth in others.

Physical virginity has about as much value as an intact appendix. It is utterly silly to make a mountain out of physical virginity while ignoring the fidelity to God, self and spouse or friend which underlies genuine chastity. It is quite ludicrous to remain virgin out of pure pride while saints who lost their virginity lived for years in moral virginity in service to God and their fellowmen. It was not the weird religious exaggerators who created the confusion around virginity. For the most peculiar reasons physical virginity always seems in the highest demand in the brides of the egocentric, selfindulgent men so responsible for the world's short supply of virgins. Even permissive society has not made it easy for such people to reconcile themselves to the promiscuity of their wives and daughters. They, of course, are the masters of the double standard, wearing the trappings of rectitude so selfrighteously despite years of constant exploitation of others.

Premarital love requires little sexual experience beyond living one's life well aware of one's own maleness or femaleness. A well functioning imagination makes the difference between the realism of the experienced and the naivety of the inexperienced. The imagination acts on the emotions nearly as realistically as does experience. Like the emotions the imagination can be used well, suppressed or exploited. The creative realist uses it well and experiences the sexual aspects of his humanity almost to the full. He clearly grasps the power of the genitals to provide incoming pleasure and pain sensations, never being deluded that such pleasure sensations can add up to personal happiness or ever be anything more than incoming sensations are. The well used imagination gives sex its rightful place in life, but more importantly it rejects completely the exaggeration of sex which causes it to be a destructive rather than a loving factor in human relationships. Through such use of the imagination chastity is able to conduct love through the shoals of sexual exploitation to loving interest in another person. It is wrong to deny the young the ability to be strong enough to do this.

When the imagination is unhappily used as a built-in pleasure pack, exploited through fantasizing and day dreaming, chastity is out and frustration and unhappiness are in. Then lust is easily identified quite incorrectly with love, one is pushed towards a harsh tyrannical meanness in personal relationships, verging on serious emotional illness. A well used imagination can make the difference between emotional health with chastity and emotional illness with lust. The understanding and courage it takes to use the imagination well is probably the greatest weapon in managing the emotion of fear, perhaps the most dominant of human emotions. Fear of rejection not only nips innumerable beginnings of love in the bud but, allowed to dominate, it robs one of his very humanity.

Since courtship is aimed at a truly loving marriage the people involved ought to give priority to integrity and personal maturity, a life time job, but made infinitely easier for beginning well. To achieve such a beginning they must see sex not merely as a source of pleasure, not merely as a process for having children and a family (which it is essentially) but a way of expressing love. But they have to be loving to express love. They must see love not as something that two people do but something that each person does. To the extent that each person loves, they will be loving. The people who succeed in achieving some degree of real love in their individual personal lives find themselves masters rather than slaves of their emotions. When they discover, as they must, that there is nothing loving about either sex or marriage, they will have the love to flow into their sexual and married lives to make those lives loving.

It is love not permissiveness which permits a man and a woman to lie together in tender proximity without having intercourse, if and when that is what love requires. But a permissive society and permissive living have made it impossible for tradition, culture or even fear to protect anyone from tragic sexual experience from which only wisdom, strength and personal love can save them. Permissiveness has made a shambles of every sex education program however well the pill, availability of contraceptives and even abortion have disguised or hidden the results. Permissiveness has hurled countless young people into hasty marriages for which they were in no way ready, climaxing relationships presumed loving until they proved merely sexual and so impossible. Surely only an affluent world no longer contending with the basics of food, shelter, clothing, health and education could make such a place for permissive sex as is the rule today, could consider such a secondary priority as a primary one. But permissiveness and easy association of the sexes can also make possible the startling discovery that most people can and many do sleep in tender, loving proximity without sexual intercourse. The genuinely loving few learn this. The unloving and presumptuous many simply never learn. For the latter, the sexual compulsion of physical proximity obliterates the road to personal closeness. Since physical proximity does not purify the heart nor separation or distance constitute virtue, those who have not attained inner closeness before enjoying physical proximity will certainly copulate.

The lust which ends up in bed does not start there. The deep, respectful, personal love of man for woman does enable him to sleep with her without sexual intercourse if such a thing is desirable for any good reason. Lust not sex is evil; chastity is not a matter of strong protective walls or segregation, but of loving. If, as many moralists have insisted, a man cannot be alone with a woman without sin, then virtue is meaningless and love a delusion. But if love of God and dedication to truth make one virtuous and loving, if chastity is indeed a way of loving deeply and well, then personal love directs both the having of sex and abstention from it, and person to person communication is a broader and a happier, a more thrilling achievement than sex could ever be. Sex, in itself, adds nothing to personal closeness and sharing but is merely one manifestation of it. If this closeness has not even begun in courtship, marriage, of itself, will not provide it.

The union of loving people can make sex superfluous when they are motivated by their actual needs rather than their felt desires. It is often more loving to forego intercourse than to have it. Doing so does not require superhuman people devoid of sexual feelings or divinely anaesthetized as many quite oblivious of the overwhelming power to love would believe. It is just that sexuality can be so integrated into one's humanity that the genital function by itself is powerless to add anything to love. Such sexual integration is experienced by anyone who loves enough. Such love is well within the human potential and many do achieve it. The genuine celibate in no way ceases to be truly male or female. Yet such a person willingly foregoes sex for long periods and even life, for a worthy reason. The power to love does control every other human function and loving people soon discover this.

Premarital loving is beset by many problems not the greatest nor least of which is sex. Those who learn to love very young as people are capable of doing, will love personally in and through sexual emergence to adulthood. They will love in their personal relationships and marriages. Courtship is merely a special time with a special motivation for beginning to love if one has not begun, or developing in love if one has already started to love. However there is nothing about courtship which is essentially loving. Freedom is a condition necessary to love. Courtship challenges young people to use that freedom to gain an understanding of and insight into the other person, including the sexual dimension, while using available protections against sexual unrealism, sexual domination.

It seemed to serve many generations well to believe the fiction that men are more highly sexed than women. For such to have been the case there would have had to be an essential difference in their humanity, when in fact they were made for each other. The fiction seemed to make chastity a little easier for the females of whom chastity seemed required culturally, and, who paid a much higher price for unchastity. Women thus had a little protection from their own lust and even some from the lust of the male. That fiction, combined with the fear of pregnancy and childbearing have now been replaced with permissiveness, contraceptives and sexual equality movements. Thus the lust which was admired in the men is becoming equally admired in the women whose goal seems to be equally as bad as the men's. Now the lust of women is as equally obvious as that of men. Women seem to be proud that they are as interested in sex as men, as sexual as men. Thus their chastity like that of men can only be acquired in the full awareness and acceptance of their sexual compulsions, that is in the battle to make their sexuality serve their power to love rather than dominate it. Premaritally it is the job of women to determine what place sex is to play in their loving, in their marriages, whether they will run sex or sex will run them. Women's liberation means that women will have to rely on their own strengths rather than the protection of the male such as it was, they have to be at least as personally loving as the men if their lives are going to be meaningful.

The real preparation for marriage, and thus for all intents and purposes for adulthood and normal life, is premarital love. There can hardly be a poorer preparation than premarital sex, not for what it is in itself but for what it says about the relationship or lack of relationship. It is only that those who cannot wait for sex cannot usually wait for anything else they momentarily feel the need of. Patience is the notable quality of the loving person for it represents the inner strength enabling one not to be easily aroused whatever the provocation. It is the quality of the person who can hear another out, whose anxiety to prepare his rebuttal is not so great as to prevent his listening. Communication is impossible with any but a patient person who has the interest and the time it takes for love and friendship. The patient person's life is based in real, lasting, well tested values. While this seems a lot to ask of young people, the happiness of their marriages depends on it. Certainly today when marriage as an institution is being questioned and doubted even though there is no real replacement for it on the horizon, young people getting married need to become the very best of friends, or at least be aware of the kind of love involved not in romantic love but in personal love, the love of friendship, the love required for a happy relationship with anyone, but especially with a husband or a wife.

If one does not learn this premaritally all is not necessarily lost. One can learn it in the crises which are part of every normal, good marriage, but it is more difficult. One can learn it later on in life as the end result of many failures, but few do. Man seems to have such a propensity for compounding his foolishness, his mistakes. Premarriage is a time of pressure to have sex; it could be made a time of pressure to understand and develop friendship and the very durable love that characterizes friendship which can stand the stress even of marriage. Certainly only genuine love can withstand the onslaught of the boredom inevitable in every marriage and especially those marriages in the contraceptive age when the thrill and presumed meaning of sex are worn out so quickly only to expose the lack of relationship between those who lived so entirely in the physical, so oblivious of the spiritual dimension where personal love really is.

No marriage ever need break up. Each person has within himself or herself the power to love. The love of one person for another is enough to make a marriage work. The love of each person for the other makes a marriage beautiful. There are two relationships in marriage, his with her, and hers with him. And they are as different as he is from her, or she from him. Each must work on his own. Whatever security there is in a marriage comes from the realism with which one works or both work. If sex is difficult to talk about love is moreso, but it can be done, and the discussion lasts forever because the material of it is as deep and lasting as the hearts and souls of man and woman. The discussion and understanding of love should start a very long time before marriage, though any time at all is better than never.

CHAPTER THIRTEEN

The Loving Married Life

Marriage ought to represent an irrevocable, exclusive, deep personal commitment to another for life, by one who considers himself obligated without recourse to contribute everything within his power to the growth and development of the other person. The problem marriage is the one in which the immature seek fulfilment in the love they want to receive and the rewards they expect to get. Mature people are ready for marriage, ready to give. One is sexually mature at twelve or fourteen years of age, but emotionally mature only when sex has been integrated into loving, that is, when one is capable of the deep, loving relationship required by marriage. This can be said only of those who have a valid set of values, including the spiritual ones. Marriage should be reserved to people who do love. One must not wait for marriage to learn to love. It was possible to do that in the past, when the institution was supported by so many cultural props not present in modern urban living. It is virtually impossible today.

The loving marriage is the most complete person-to-person relationship. But few people who have not learned to love before marriage do so after. When the excitement of infatuation and sex fulfilment dies down and the novelty of both wears off, very little relationship between the people is discovered. Marriage does offer loving people a better opportunity for a deeper relationship than simple friendship because it includes the full use of the sexual dimension with a valid exclusiveness and fuller union. However the use people make of that opportunity depends entirely on the degree to which they are truly loving, which has precious little to do with marriage in itself. Loving people so relate in marriage as to pool their resources in common creative interests. They have, when truly loving, such security that the good of others never threatens their own. From the strength of their unthreatened love they share themselves with others, primarily their children. And children are essential to a loving marriage. To a loving couple a childless marriage is a frustration, to be solved by adoption or investment of themselves in the equivalent of a family.

A loving marriage is the human completion of man in both the sexual and personal senses. It is the actual full equation of the good of a special person with one's own. This unfortunately is not true of most marriages, not through any defect in the institution, but through the fault of the people. Being a social animal, man not only needs others, but procreates them through his closest personal association in love—marriage. Because man's need of others is much more personal than sexual, love in marriage is far more important than sex. Sex in marriage works best in the loving production of people, that is in the loving production of each other, for each other. The "I-thou" relationship so fundamentally needed by man can produce the kind of society in which man is most fully at home. In such a society man's primary and most vital relationship is not mere physical coupling but a union of whole people at their very mature best.

When marriage means love, rather than a licence to copulate, its preservation as an institution will be assured. Man has come a long way from the days when love in marriage was a luxury and children a necessity. With progress in science man has more control of his material destiny, and must develop the love required for his fulfilment as a human being. Love is now necessary for a happy marriage.

Children today seldom contribute to the material security or physical comfort of parents, but, on the contrary, are to a large extent a discomfort, a burden and responsibility, calling for greater parental love and dedication. Previously, they were required to help with the material establishment of the family and provide its food and protection, and as replacements for those taken by death and sickness and other then unavoidable disasters. Although pensions and insurance cannot replace children as emotional security in old age, they have replaced them as financial security.

One no longer has to raise six children so that two will survive adolescence, and one of those willingly support the parents in their old age. Since parents now not only survive, but survive much longer, they provide for their own old age. Thus there is pressure to have fewer children and provide better for themselves. Parents now must mean more to each other.

Modern parents outlive their basic responsibility to their children, and thus parents who were busily occupied with children for many years generally find themselves alone with each other when the children are established on their own. They surprisingly discover that they hardly know each other. In their concern and busyness about the children they never developed a personal relationship and so find themselves virtual strangers, often both uninterested and uninteresting. When the love so vital in marriage today is needed most, it simply does not exist because there has been no concerted effort to achieve it.

The public, which took for granted an automatic love relationship in marriage, must now realize that such a relationship must be studied and worked at if it is to exist. Love is not always easy or pleasurable but it is always possible. Freer than he ever was from all but the sexual pressure to marry, man must accept that sexual attraction is the poorest basis on which to build a marriage. The sexual relationship is not necessarily a loving one and, in itself, seldom leads to love. Scientists can present and explain the purely mechanical aspects of the genital function and still do nothing for love, and therefore nothing really vital to help unhappy marriages. People who have little to say to each other before marriage will find, after a very few years of marriage with few children or none, that they still have nothing to say to each other and sex itself has become a dull bore. There is no relationship at all. One should only marry one with whom it is joy to share ideas, thoughts and plans, and who is capable of a relationship far exceeding the sexual.

Negatively sex-dominated moralists have left a legacy of misguided notions of both lust and love. The mere having of children was made a virtue, whether they were conceived, born and raised in love or in negligence. Lust is as destructive of love in marriage as out of it. In the loving marriage there is certainly the power to direct sex to the thoughtful, loving conception of children. Those who will not control their sex appetites are poor lovers and even poorer parents, simply because they are incapable of the concern for others which is love.

Children ought never to be the accidental result of the uncontrolled passion of parents. Though deeply loving people do generally want the children they conceive, few accept that they need only have the children they want, or that the sexual function can be directed to that end simply because it is under the same controls as any of man's powers, which are less than himself. The conception of children should be considered a privilege. Children are new people to be brought, by loving parents, into a world critically short of people willing to share their love with others. Certainly, the intricate planning, fantastic calculations and incredible costs of space exploration invalidate the contention that the thoughtful, loving conception of children by man is too difficult a challenge. But this contention must persist as long as people prefer the pleasure of sex to its purpose, on which the pleasure is based. The progress of man, in love as in all things, depends on the dedicated goodness of the few who inspire its miracles.

The primary, but by no means exclusive, purpose of sex is the loving production of a family. Marriage is an obstacle to the sterile pseudo-love between people with no interest whatever in fruit from their love. The loving marriage must be fruitful in children because real love is of its essence creative. Any partner is eternally grateful to a deceased spouse who thoughtfully left the living with an inheritance of happy memories and a fruitful love. Money is a disappointing substitute for the living legacy of loving children witnessing the love that was. They can be provided only by people whose relationship is deeper than money or possessions, whose lives are lived in mutual interest and the loving service of a happy marriage, in a home made joyful and alive with loving people. In a culture in which this concept becomes obsolete, marriage must lose its meaning and become merely a licence for people to cohabitate in respectable sterility. Marriage, for far too many people, is a legal service to assure equitable distribution of the spoils on dissolution of a contract, the duration of which is as predictable as the people signing it.

The drug addiction currently laying waste the human resources of the affluent society is merely the beginning of the harvest of unhappiness being reaped in the unloved children of a sick society. Children conceived and born unloved are just as crippled as the thalidomide babies of the recent drug scandal. When they are reared in neglect, the future of such children is indeed bleak. The social philosophers who, in typical oversimplification, recommend contraceptives to insure against unloved babies contribute nothing to the development of loving people. However accepted, rationalized or justified, the use of contraceptives does nothing to bring loving within the reach of man. They are, at best, the lesser of evils. No one enjoys using them. When love is properly understood children can be conceived, born and reared in love, rather than as an accident of sexual indulgence or through complete indifference to the responsibility of parenthood.

It is ridiculous to think that sexually indulgent, pleasure-oriented people can suddenly become loving and self-sacrificing when they decide that they are ready to conceive and bear a child. Such people conceive their children as projections of their own egos, and seldom respect the person or the rights of the children themselves, as the legalization of abortion so clearly indicates. Those people who promote abortion, rejecting the full rights of the foetus, will not respect the personal rights of the newborn infants either, but will use them for their own satisfaction. To "feel" the need for children is not sufficient reason for conceiving them without the will to love them. Our affluent, emotionally crippled world is full of children prostituted to the projected ambitions of parents, who, unable to inspire the respect of their children, bribe them for it with indulgences. Parents who bribe their children for affection are oblivious to the proper growth and development of the children, which requires parental unwillingness to spoil them.

The current shortsightedness of the abortion solution to unwanted children is incredible in civilized society. Hardly a voice is heard to question the sexual irresponsibility creating the pregnancy. It is indeed an Alice-in-Wonderland society which will respect "No Parking" signs, support civil rights, and deplore child massacres in wartime, and poverty and hunger in the underdeveloped nations, while its youngest citizens (foetuses of less than twenty weeks) are flushed down hospital drains, too young to hire a lawyer or appeal to the United Nations, a mere ten weeks from the full protection of the law. Criminals and hoodlums indeed fare better in that society.

Premarital intercourse is probably no more damaging than being raised in a puritan, antisexual atmosphere which implies that sex is an unnatural, uncontrollable monster. But despite the permissive extravagance of behavioural scientists, there is no solid evidence that premarital intercourse has any inherent value. In fact, the evidence is against anticipating marital privileges without assuming marriage obligations, if one wishes to be happy. Love cannot be bought with a credit card. However, it should surprise no one that the society which rejects almost all restraint on any other pleasurable emotion, also rejects sexual restraint. When "doing your thing" is stupidly identified with doing as you feel like doing, rather than with making every effort to reach your potential as a human being, few are willing to admit that controlling one's sexual appetites is at least possible, and even more necessary than controlling one's temper. Marriage is no remedy for uncontrollable sexual desires, which are not always or easily satisfied in marriage. Uncontrolled urges wreck any relationship, and marriage tolerates few delusions about sex. The miracle of self-control, so essential to love, does not descend on the undisciplined person by the fact of marriage. A successful married life requires sexual discipline as much as success in business requires work discipline. It should be noted that those who make discipline easy by eliminating normal sexual emotions from their lives form the harmful habit of avoiding other unpleasant realities, and make it almost impossible to relate to others realistically as love requires.

The worthwhile sexual relationship in marriage is experienced in the worthwhile personal relationship. The easily aroused man may be momentarily stimulating but he is impossible to live with, and marriage is living together in love. The married couple should be first of all good friends. Incredible as it seems, any number of well educated, materially successful, physically attractive adults find themselves unable to discuss many aspects of their personal lives with their spouses. The idea that people who share the same bed for years, and appear easily before each other in their physical nakedness, will automatically appear easily before each other in the naked intimacy of their emotional and personal lives is quite erroneous. Only those who have the full acceptance of the other in love can do this, since love alone creates enough security to risk misunderstanding. Too many are content to let their marriage stagnate in a relatively pleasant sexual relationship often personally meaningless. Sex plays an exaggerated role in their lives because they are afraid to communicate more than can be disguised with a passionate kiss; they are afraid of any penetration deeper than that of sexual intercourse. Awareness of another as a body is in no way awareness of another as a person. The delightful security of those whose relationship can surely survive misunderstandings is the basis for communication. The depth of love in any marriage can be correctly gauged by the actual communication between the parties.

Loving marriage is the union of people who understand each other. Generally troubled marriages are between immature, insecure people who primarily "feel" they love each other but admittedly do not understand each other, have made little or no studied effort to understand each other, and generally do not have a clue as to what understanding involves, let alone the courage or purpose to undertake it. They speak without conversing, and "communication" means only reassurance for themselves, rather than understanding of the other. For insecure people, understanding always means agreement, rather than awareness of how the other person thinks and feels regardless of agreement or disagreement. Understanding of another comes with the eagerness to hear and the desire to ponder, which is beyond people who talk all the time, who fear to listen and dread thinking because they cannot risk disillusionment. Such people may be legally married but they are not lovingly married; they are capable of sharing their bodies in intercourse but not their personhood in understanding. Acceptance in so many marriages depends on the degree to which the couple do not know each other, or worse, the degree to which they are able to deceive each other. So many of them quite truthfully say, "I could never tell my wife or husband that," expressing exactly the very limited dimensions of their love.

Love cannot be expected to mature in a marriage in which neither party has the self-respect, or desire, to continue growing as a person. The allure of most wives after the second child or a few years of marriage is about equal to the chivalry of their husbands. Being bored to death is a hard way to die, and boredom is the fate of married people refusing to make themselves interesting as people, and inspiring to their partners. Surely the job of being personally attractive is worthy of as much effort as the job of being physically attractive. Those whose understanding and use of beauty aids is restricted to commercial products and plastic surgery, have no appreciation of genuine personal beauty, or the virtues which keep the heart young and love fresh. A constant growth in goodness and deepening of integrity by both people make marriage a wonderful relationship and give both the partners a continuing sense of privilege.

External compulsion to persist in a marriage in which there is no relationship between the people, or when it is realized that there was no real marriage in the first place, has caused thoughtful people to rebel against an irrevocable decision being made, in a highly emotional situation under considerable sexual compulsion, to enter a relationship with so many more dimensions than sex. The obvious, and too easy, answer is trial marriage with contraceptives. Although this cop-out appals because of its unrealism, any mistake seems preferable to emotionally crippled children born of a meaningless union which is farcically maintained because public morality or public order apparently demands it. The answer surely is not to make a farce out of marriage but to insist that people qualify for marriage by learning to love.

The unloving married relationship exists because the people in it will not love. They have the power to do so, if they wish to use it. Their problem is like that of the alcoholic. They must first recognize the problem, admit it and then do what has to be done — learn to love. Almost any marriage can be made to work if the parties have the goodwill basic to the loving relationship. The marriage in which love has "died" can be resurrected if the partners will learn to love instead of running away to begin the same disappointing process with other partners as immature as themselves. It takes honesty and courage to see and admit the loveless marriage, but that same honesty and courage make love possible between those willing to seek help from good friends or competent counselors with valid convictions about love, personal relationships and marriage.

Counselors, like psychiatrists, are a mixed bag. Their competence demands the conviction that love directs sex to the production of the loving family in which happily married people are deeply invested, and of which they are very protective. The prophets of the new morality rightly insist that functional sex and the preservation of the species do not require marriage. However, love and the development of the human potential to love, do. Marriage is merely the commitment of those sufficiently loving to direct their lives through sex to the personal union which welcomes children and supplies the milieu for their basic emotional health. Counselors who do not see marriage as the commitment underlying the secure atmosphere in which lovers can grow personally are more a menace than a help. Such counselors lack the artistic imagination to explain the value of stable marriage in the development of the partners as people.

Learning to love requires imagination, the ability and eagerness to see ahead and plan for the future with enough flexibility to include the wishes and aspirations of another person. The imagination can present an authentic picture of the happy loving marriage, the qualities to develop in oneself and to seek in one's partner, the joys to be expected in companionship and sharing, the goodwill and personal costs they require. The lack of imagination, or the poorly directed imagination is largely responsible for the false picture of undiluted happiness which many young lovers accept without question as they go blithely into marriage. Their ultimate disillusionment in each other and in marriage could have been prevented by the studied application of the imagination to their prospective relationship, well before marriage. The imagination previews the realities of marriage and outlines the adequate personal preparation. The competent counselor does the same, if the imagination has not. But he himself must be convinced of the potential for love in everyone, and refuse to see personal failures as defects in the institution of marriage.

Marriage counselors are plagued with people lacking the imagination which makes understanding possible, and love a reality. Sex and its overrated pleasure, mistaken emphasis on minor factors in personal relating, can ultimately revolt both parties in a marriage. When one is all fired up for making love and the other completely enervated from a hopeless day at the office, or in the home, neither understanding the needs of the other, there is no place to go. Some imagination would make it plain that there are burdens to be disposed of, and understanding to be given and received, if the sharing of bodies is to truly represent the sharing of lives. People, capable of personal relationships, who begin by sharing their bodies in love can go on to deeper, mutual interest and genuine personal concern for the other. However, the union of bodies being so easy and superficially rewarding, most unions tend to stop there. If so, lack of imagination and interested effort to explore each other in depth bankrupt love before communication is ever established. After mutual sexual exploitation, the marriage is like a worked-out mine, leaving the exploiters to separate in their search for other fields to conquer.

The economic crises of marriage, which, counselors seem to agree, form about 30% of all marriage problems, require great imaginative understanding simply because the male and female approaches to the economy of home and family are so different. The understanding agreement required for raising a family also requires tremendous imaginative thought and disciplined planning, made possible by the foresight and vision flowing from a developed imagination. Evidence of the unimaginativeness of man lies in his unquestioning will to spend eighteen or twenty years of his life qualifying himself academically for a money-earning job to pay for his marriage and the raising of a family, while refusing to spend even a small part of that time learning to love, his very reason for existing. This will continue to be the situation as long as people refuse to see that the highest human fulfilment consists in loving, and that marriage is the ideal situation for the deepest interpersonal relationships.

Because marriage is usually dominated more by sex than by love, many are unhappy about its indissolubility. They consider that marriages ought to be considered valid only between contracting parties who are indeed genuinely loving people. These are the only people capable of such a commitment. Love is the essence of Christian marriage because love is what Christianity is all about, however forgotten or unnoticed that may be. As the unloving person can be Christian in name only, the loveless marriage can be Christian in form, but certainly not in substance. Divorce, however, by no means assures that a broken marriage will be followed by a happy one, unless by some miracle the people become loving in the meantime. Realistic canonical marriage legislation should permit only loving people to enter a relationship expected to endure. Certainly, those willing to study and develop the great human potential to love can make happy and lasting marriages. Unloving people are not eligible for Christian marriage. Education, especially sex education, which was really Christian would make that clear. Love cannot be guaranteed in Christian marriage unless the marriage takes place between people who are first of all real Christians. There is nothing wrong with marriage as an institution which love cannot cure. To fail to love is not only to lack real faith and scoff at God, but it is to lack the very qualities which led to every notable human achievement. It surely is ridiculous to accept years of work as basic for education while expecting to "fall" into meaningful love.

Married love is always beautiful, because love is a marvellous achievement inseparable from the happiness of man. Married love is that very image of God seen in those beautiful people, contentedly interdependent and independent after fifty years of marriage, capable of being and living alone because they are secure enough to give each other the glorious opportunity to love fully, freely. They are whole people presenting to each other nearly unlimited horizons for loving and giving. They share great understanding with celibates because they see love as God in their midst: dependent on God, they cannot see their love enduring if cut off from God, its source. They find it easy to believe in God and to accept immortality because the love they share is so obviously a spiritual and indestructible thing, originating in, and destined for, endurance in a spiritual and eternal sphere. Despite the inevitable deterioration of the body, love for them remains essentially ageless, young, fresh and expectant. They have no sense of their love dying, and accept death as something restricted to the body. They are the antithesis of loveless people who have as little to live for as to die for.

The difference between married and single loves is purely sexual. The common factor is love. In marriage only love keeps sex from taking the lover's mind away from the person of the loved one. Single love puts such emphasis on the person that sex cannot intrude on the relationship. The same degree of love which keeps sex in its place in marriage keeps sex in its place in single male female relationships. Without that love all human relationships are meaningless charades.

CHAPTER FOURTEEN

Extramarital Love.

Love of God and of man, is the mark of the mature person. Christian celibates, whose influence in Western civilization was so great, tended to encourage ignorance and fear of human love, which they too often erroneously identified with sex. They feared that sex was a devil, a roaring lion waiting to devour them, and indeed their fear was supported with much real-life evidence. For these people, ignorance seemed desirable, what they did not know did not hurt them. Their failure to relate wholesomely to the opposite sex assured their immaturity; their effort to relate on a purely personal, asexual basis was unreal. A friend was a nice person with whom a nice personal relationship was possible and desirable. Gladly overlooked was the fact that persons come only in male and female dimensions. When, through genuine naivety or direct miscalculation, these friends eventually discovered their own maleness or femaleness, they were often unable to cope with the situation. The relationship was just too hot to handle. Thus, many simply capitulated to the normal sexual pressures and opted out of their celibate commitments.

While this does not surprise too many people, the reverse situation prevailing in marriage comes as the great surprise. Married people, quite aware of the sexual dimension, too seldom negotiate the sexual to the personal dimension. The sexual too easliy dominates the personal. Friends who related as boy and girl often married as man and woman, but never made it beyond the sexual to the basic personal relationship. When sooner or later they found their relationship essentially lacking, it rarely dawned on them that it was because it was restricted to the sexual dimension, assuring their disappointment and dissatisfaction as people.

Not understanding the real nature of the problem, these people felt bored with each other. They began consciously or more often, unconsciously to look for someone else, someone new, someone exciting. Things might have been different had they accepted that love was not sexual but personal, and, in marriage, that only the genital relationship can be exclusive, that the personal must never be. Married people must not limit their love to each other. They must know and love others too in such a way that the personal dominates the sexual, which, though always present, plays its real role, a minor one.

Many social scientists see the problem but miss the answer. They attack marriage as being too demanding, too restrictive. It is obvious to them that one needs much more than one person with whom to share oneself. Man is social. While married to one, he must love many, and, if Christian, all.

No two people relate equally, for they are different individuals. Most relationships are dominated by one person or the other. The growth element in their loving may come more in their relationships to others than to each other. If marriage was a one-to-one exclusive relationship, what place would the children and the love they require have? Where would the love of neighbour, which religion and society demand, enter the picture? The erroneous restriction of love to marriage and the labelling of extramarital love, rather than sex, as immoral have contributed greatly to the rejection of the institution of marriage. Real marriage ought not to be indentured labour. This is the message from the misguided communal marriages in the vain attempt to insist on the freedom of their love. The mistake in communes has been the brainwashing by the social revolutionaries and the media that sex is the dominant factor in marriage rather than just one of the many ways that married people can truly express their love for each other. In a healthy marriage it is, in fact one of the minor ways.

Unfortunately the genital is consistently considered intimate rather than mechanical and functional. It is too readily and wrongly identified with personal. By and large it is about as mechanical a function as humans have. Because the fittings for intercourse are relatively visible and tangible, it is too easily overlooked that people are made much more to love each other than to copulate. Because people are more obviously physical than spiritual, they tend to relate sexually more readily than they relate lovingly.

But to love is the challenge, the maturity, the wonder, and, of course, the happiness.

Few seem to realize that the "passion", "French", "deep", or "soul kiss", whatever one chooses to call the insertion of one's tongue into the mouth of another, expresses the desire to get into the life and being of another person, not merely into the body. The same thing can be said for sexual intercourse in which the penis never seems to be long enough. Intercourse always ends in the too-short satisfaction of a letdown, falling away, a disappointment, a coming apart, the failure to penetrate more deeply into the person, the inability to take the other person right into one's life. The true lover wants more than anything else to be part of the other, to enter into the very life of the other in a union more intimate, more lasting, more meaningful and fulfilling than the sexual act, of itself, can ever be. He wants to love rather than merely copulate. The failure to accept this principle leads the homosexual to genital rather than personal expression of love. The overemphasis of sex and its "per se" meaning tends to make marriages more restrictive of love than they ought to be.

Insecure people exaggerate the importance of marriage in their lives. They use it desperately to tie another person inescapably to themselves. They dread aloneness. They want someone "of their very own". They want to belong to someone. Such marriages tend to degenerate into slavery of one form or another. It is this destructive possessiveness that is repudiated by moderns discarding "legal" marriage. They need the little identity they have. They sense that being legally bound together does not so easily lead to a personal relationship. They want to keep their options open to avoid being smothered. This natural desire for wider fields than marriage stems from a dim awareness of the nature of true love which will not be restricted.

The rationale for communal marriage mistakes the social nature of man, which forbids his being tied exclusively to one person, with the priority one's relationship to another demands for children and family. Marriage can never be permitted to smother, inhibit or exclude good, healthy relationships with others. It does not happen in good marriages. The loving person excludes no one from his life, nor does another in his life militate against his fidelity in marriage. The very quality in a lover that prevents his exploitation of others, sexual or otherwise, assures fidelity in his love. The unfaithful married person is dishonourable, covetous, lustful, egocentric. Communal marriage is merely a copout from the exclusive possessiveness of a poor marriage. It is an evasion of the responsibility of the truly loving marriage rather than an extension of one's strong love to others who need its protection, help and inspiration.

Unhappily, courtship in modern society leads young people to marry people they want rather than to whom they choose to give themselves without strings. This is surely an anti-love approach to marriage. It is self-seeking. The solution to restrictive and possessive marriages is not adultery and promiscuity, but the development of healthy, loving relationships with many other people before and during marriage. This demands the genuineness, bigness and trust essential to a happy marriage, a secure marriage. Truly loving extramarital relationships take nothing away from a marriage, but add a dimension to it, a dimension essential to its survival, a wider sharing of true love. Such relationships are an anti-boredom serum, for boredom can only exist where the challenge to share is missing. The sharing dimension is essential to the personal growth of married people. Sharing is the principle so grossly misunderstood by the proponents of "free marriage". These people use the sharing dimension of true love as their excuse for extramarital sexual relationships, so exciting but so personally meaningless. One does share oneself when one loves, but sexual fidelity assures that it is one's person one shares rather than one's genital urges one indulges. Sharing is always for the good of the other rather than for the sensual satisfaction of oneself or the other.

True personal love is more difficult than mere marriage. It takes a bigger, better person to love well than to remain faithful in marriage through fear, pride, respect for convention or the demands of a good image, or even "for the sake of the children". True marital fidelity is a personal rather than legal fidelity. It is based on integrity, virtue, strength, things that preclude exploiting others or shirking responsibility. That strength makes extramarital relationships possible, relationships that do not involve cheating on marriage, but are rather the best evidence of the secure high quality marriage. Emotionally stable people attract good friends and bring fine people together in a warm social life and worthwhile social causes. The joy such people experience in sharing their lives with others moderates their need to share their bodies sexually.

Unsatisfied by sharing their bodies, their wealth and other possessions, they share *themselves* with a goodwill that protects rather than exploits others. Only such people develop true community. Their well-tried and proven judgment is excellent. They have discipline, strength and the ability to live with their most tumultuous feelings. Their wisdom makes plain just what can and must be shared and what simply cannot be shared without either failing those to whom they already relate in love, or going against a valid set of ethics on which society depends.

The "religious" or cultural marriage with the heavy accent on *fidelity* can be too big a load for the victims of those who use marital chains with ruthless selfishness. Fidelity, like all virtue is not compelled but freely acquired. The slavery of such oppressive marriages seems a boon only to those immature and unstable people incapable of extramarital relationships. Such people, unfortunately, may be the majority.

People capable of extramarital relationships are those who are the beneficiaries rather than the victims of their experience. Having once put their hands on a hot stove, they neither make the same mistake again, nor do they live in terror of stoves, hot or cold. They share the loves and friendships of their married partners without delusions, naivety or a double standard. They accept and appreciate the feelings of others about the partner of their choice. Extramarital love requires an understanding of and ability to handle guilt feelings. These feelings must be seen and acknowledged as the reaction to disapproval of one's peers whose suspicions betray prejudices, jealousy, limited horizons and little real virtue. Handling them well requires rare finesse and high goodness possessed only by strong-principled people. Slaves to the approval of others simply do not have these qualities.

The ability of married people to share their extramarital loves and friendships depends on their basic goodness and the genuineness of their mutual love. Those few people who in marriage are great and good friends relate on such a plane of basic honesty and mutual interest that their trust is valid and warranted, never naive. Sharing their loves with each other, they need no escape to fantasy land.

The sane, thoughtful celibate often relates better than married people to the opposite sex. His approach tends to be personal rather than sexual. He lives comfortably with his maleness (or in the case of the female, her femaleness), neither avoiding it nor living as if it did not exist. Moving realistically through the sexual to the personal makes for a degree of trust and understanding arrived at much earlier than is normally the case between male and female. Still, it is equally the case with the loving husband or wife, who, sexually satisfied with his partner to whom he or she is personally, not merely legally, faithful, relates quite easily and comfortably on a personal basis with those of the opposite sex. A plane of communication above and beyond the playing of games is quickly reached. It makes for friendships of a depth and intensity all too rare. Such friendships are not hidden, furtive, frightened. They can stand the glare of realistic examination and withstand the suspicions of the envious. They are beyond anyone denying their possibility. Those capable of them are rarely conned by the players of games. Not always, but generally, married people who do not have loving relationships with each other, need more personal growth and development before they are ready for extramarital friendship and love.

Despite appreciable evidence to the contrary marriage is still the state in which deep, personal, male-female love is best nurtured and developed. This is not so for those people for whom marriage means stereo-typed, ecclesiastically blessed or government-registered union of man and woman for life, with the expectation of automatic love to follow. Marriage may produce the opportunity for love but never the substance of love. Modern marriage must be the challenge to expand rather than restrict one's love, something very much at variance with the elimination of children in the marriages.

Alarmists fear the imminent passing of what has been too generally accepted as marriage. With all the currently acceptable personal and social outs, if a marriage is to persist, it must be loving. People in marriage are never genuinely loving with each other if they are not also loving with others outside their marriage. A marriage remains intact and happy primarily because of the highly developed power of the partners to love with a love not restricted to each other but productive of happy relationships with others.

Current social developments offer little encouragement to love extramaritally. Until recently women generally had too little to say about whom they married. They had no alternative but to settle with the designated or available husband, like it or not, make the best of things in raising a family and keeping a home. If they did not like it they had no place to go, no means of support. However, with women now in the working force, better educated and much more in demand by technology, there are many alternatives to the stereotype marriage. Again, the pill, has enabled most women to escape the unwanted burden of numerous children to whom they were unwillingly tied by the minimal sense of decency. Permissiveness has reached outstanding proportions; easy divorce is readily available and becoming by the day less financially, socially and emotionally costly. These factors make genuine love essential in the pursuit of marital happiness. Genuine love is the power to relate well to many people while remaining faithful to one's obligations, especially the marriage bond. A love so strong that it can function extramaritally is required to preserve marriage today and enable people to preserve their integrity in a society where extramarital sex is socially acceptable, even a requirement, for those who feel compelled to prove their liberation from every restraint and even from virtue itself. Permissiveness is the poorest preparation for extramarital love based on genuine concern for others. But a free society presents a great challenge to the growth that makes extramarital love possible. In the past, the censure of others in a closed society intimidated even the brave, while driving the coward to seek furtively what he had not the courage to seek openly.

The enlightenment and wisdom to know what is right and the virtue to do it are the qualities required of the person who really loves another while remaining, not merely technically, but personally faithful to his marriage obligations. His fidelity must be his own conviction and choice, and not come from external pressure. It must be a matter of personal integrity not merely pride in his own good image.

There are many people who would not steal another man's money who would not think twice of having an affair with his wife, if she were willing and there was no real threat of being caught. Such people are completely incapable of extramarital love, which is quite at odds with misappropriation of the assets of another. The genuine interest of the lover in the good of the other is what enables him to place his own assets at the disposal of the other according to the need, not the want of that other. Love distinguishes readily between needs and wants. The loving person is equally able to resist being exploited as to resist exploiting. He just does not permit the assets of one he loves to be plundered by the unbridled desires of an intruder, however attractive. He is very hard to deceive in this matter, because the outgoing nature of his love renders him all but immune to greed and lust. Because of these qualities the emotional cost of being married to such a person is more than compensated for by the security and trust generated by his love. That such a condition is ideal does not take away from its reality. The general denial of the reality of such relationships comes mainly from the division of people into the exploiters and the fearful, those unwilling to love and those unable to. The loving are neither. Extramarital loving will remain impossible to those hung up on the fetish that love comes through sexual compatibility. Anyone so immature and naive as to believe that sexual compatibility could possibly be the magic gateway to good and great relationships never gets to the personal relationship, never really loves personally. The fact is that there will always be sexual compatibility where there is genuine love. The cure for frigidity or impotence is not teaching people to copulate but to love. Granted, it is a more difficult undertaking, but real cures always are. When people have completed the various sensitivity courses and psychological treatment for their hangups, if they have not learned to love, all they really have is a mechanical ability to enjoy themselves through the unrewarding exploitation of another. That the other is willingly exploited only indicates that both are equally hung up, crippled.

In a marriage in which there is sexual compatibility but little or no love, the minimal personal relationship that exists is lived on a dominantly emotional level with such incredible mood variations that the marriage sooner or later becomes intolerable. The fragile relationships existing in such marriages simply cannot sustain extramarital love, which conflicts with rather than complements the marriage relationship. Yet it is people in these marriages who generally promote extramarital relationships, as escape routes from boredom. Needless to say, the end results of their efforts are so bad that they negate the very concept of extramarital loving. Only the extraordinarily good marriage can support extramarital love. In the extraordinarily good marriage there is always a great outflow of love into extramarital relationships, which do not drain but in turn feed the bases from which they flow, much as the veins return the blood to the heart.

Extramarital love depends entirely on the spiritual depths of the love, not on deluded spirituality but real spirituality. People whose main aim in it, is the flight from pain or the pursuit of pleasure see that love as a totally emotional involvement rather than as the most deeply spiritual act or state possible to man. This is not a spirituality that negates the inherent sexuality of man, but one that contains that sexuality. It is through this spirituality that man can love God Himself, Who is a purely spiritual being, and love that God even more than he loves his own life. Obviously such love is beyond the pain—or pleasure—dominated person. Needless to say, the emotion-dominated person could never accept love as the unexciting, constant force it is, unthreatened by the greatest trial, turmoil or unpleasantness, something that persists through feelings of deepest hurt or burning hate, a constant of the greatest force. The love capable of extramarital relationships is like the large mass of ocean water. Emotional love is like the passing storms on that water that sooner or later subside, leaving the large mass as it was, largely undisturbed. Married love incapable of living with the normal emotional stresses of any normal marriage surely cannot sustain the stress of extramarital love. That is primarily because of the shallowness of the married love. And if this is so in normal circumstances, it surely is much moreso in the day of the working wife and her free association with other men, the day of the childless marriage, the almost limitless availability of attractive people of the opposite sex in stimulating circumstances, in various stages of undresss and deliberate familiarity. Yet the genuine love able to survive these situations and grow can sustain and profit by extramarital relationships, which test and strengthen love.

When one of the married partners relates well to a third party of the opposite sex, the situation is too generally neither seen for what it really is, nor understood for its real significance, nor accepted for what it could be, a broadening of love and a greater challenge to deeper personal relating. Too few think the situation through, but jump too hastily to the conclusion that irreconcilable differences have arisen. In pique and its pain they tend to split prematurely. The slightest competition or threat to their position is intolerable. Their separation when it takes place merely clears the way for the same experience with another equally immature person in a relationship doomed to end as abruptly and stupidly as the last one. The basic principle is that genuine love tolerates and contains all other genuinely loving relationships. Genuine lovers do live constantly with the feelings of threat, which they interpret correctly and endure well, for in coping well with them their love grows stronger.

It is impossible to love *too much*. That is a contradiction in terms. What is meant usually by that expression is that one has made a mess of one's relationships by being too naive, too indulgent, too blind to reality, simply misguided. The *felt* factors, the least important ones, are given too great emphasis in our emotion-dominated culture. When love is not *felt* one tends too quickly and easily to deny its existence. One can have a far greater love for someone who, through years of familiarity and acceptance, bores one, than one has for an intensely exciting newly found acquaintance in a relationship of no depth whatever. But that principle will be neither recognized nor accepted as long as love is identified with the superficial excitement rather than the unfelt depth of the relationship. Only the most meaningful and genuine love can negotiate the boredom and loneliness experienced by everyone, however loving, in the years of test and crisis that lie along the route of true marital love. Poets notwithstanding, everyman is an island. He is born alone and he dies alone. He was not made by or for any other human being, but by and for God alone. Only God will ever satisfy him completely. It is not that other human beings lack something essential to their humanity. It is just that they never had to offer what man wants most, needs most—total happiness, total fulfilment. The truest human relationship leaves man at some time and some place, alone with his God. This is the only real explanation of man's universal and constant preoccupation with God. There has to be something tragically comical about the atheist arguing so vehemently about someone he really believes just isn't there. It is through his loving relationship with the God of love that man learns the spirituality of love, and how to love his fellowman for what he is, faithfully, truly, and universally.

No one who depends on excitement and joyous companions will ever love well. He will not use the time alone that he needs to learn to live with himself. And the man who cannot live *with* himself will not live with another but *off* that other. By the same token, no one whose security in a relationship depends on keeping all other love out of his or her life will ever love truly, simply because he has become too dependent on the other, does in fact live *off* that other. Anyone who loves accepts without question any other who is genuinely good for the loved one. This kind of married love takes all limits off love while insuring its fidelity. The boundless security of such love reflects beautifully the love of God from which all love comes.

The love that panics in the face of boredom and loneliness never existed. Excitement sought consciously, or more often, unconciously, to banish the fear that love has proven fickle or never really existed, indicates emotional domination and hardcore selfishness. For such people a new face coming over the horizon, showing interest, starts excitement off and running. There is suddenly, once more, something to live for, "joie de vivre". There is new pleasure, a thrill too easily mistaken for happiness. "Good" married people do feel terribly guilty about such experiences, which they tend to mishandle in one of two ways. They either tend to suppress their feelings, which they rationalize or hide even from themselves, and then get in over their heads, or they tend to withdraw to the security of the emotionally unrewarding marriage. They feel guilt, resentment and depression, which becomes unbearable in an already threatened relationship. They should have accepted this whole experience as a challenge to begin to love, to really make something of a relationship going nowhere. At this point their marriage, which is hardly more than a legal thing, could begin to be a personally loving thing, if they would only work at it, if they would only begin to trust each other, start to communicate and share.

Such a delightful experience can be a disaster for the immature. The other side of the fence does indeed look very, very green. The tougher it is to live maturely with the existing relationship, their marriage, the more realistic and entrancing looks the escape over the fence to the promising land. There is seldom any turning back from here. These people are no longer believers. The course is set, irreversible and destructive; it leads from one disaster to another. Such need not be the case if the people in the marriage will grow up, level with each other, and plan the course of their love. At this point, love, as always, has only one demand, one essential—the will to do everything possible for the good of any and all loved.

Faced with a new situation, a new person, a new relationship the deadliest thing one can do is contrast the crushing experience of living the present marriage with the imagined delights of living the mirage relationships. It is utterly unrealistic to compare known dullness to unknown delight. Everything about the current situation feels wrong and everything about the anticipated one feels right and always wonderfully promising. The real burden of the present makes it easy to accept that "nothing could be worse than the situation I am in". How many have used this as the rationale for jumping out of the frying pan into the fire! Present pain is always more acute than the pain of the past or of the future. Disaster could be avoided if one could only accept that anyone not loving well in the current situation will hardly improve in the new one. There is no magic in a new situation. The only real magic is in loving well, genuinely. There is much hard work to be done. To imagine otherwise is indeed fantasy. It surely is very hard work to negotiate and live extramarital love. Why does such a simple truth elude so many? If one already has good relationships with those he loves, he will probably have them with others.

One does not run around seeking extramarital love. It is encountered in the normal course of an already loving life. Obviously, lonely, unfulfilled, unhappy people leading empty lives are not in any way disposed to be objective about attractive people coming into range. They are much too desperate for relief from present woes. In fact they clutch newcomers to themselves lest they escape. They are constantly searching for victims. It takes happy people relating well in the situations in which they are already living to offer others the opportunity and conditions for genuine extramarital love.

Extramarital love is not the usual experience of young married people. It is not that the young do not love, but rather that their love is not normally mature enough to sustain a new, intricate love relationship. Nor have they achieved from their meagre experience the wisdom required for extramarital love.

It is all but impossible to tell young people in love that they hardly know what real love means. Yet most people married for several years will readily admit that when they were married they hardly knew each other, let alone loved. Extramarital love is for those people who appreciate the personal dimension and have had considerable experience with it. Extramarital love is for man and woman at their best, and their best is far above the delusion that the sexual must conquer all, far above the delusion that the sexual has anything to offer people unless it comes from the personal love underlying it. Personally mature people have long ago accepted that sex is not so vital that life without it is impossible, nor so essential that love without it is impossible.

The very term "extramarital", has from common usage, taken on a connotation of wrongness when combined with the word "love". It is as if it could only refer to an "affair", some kind of sordid romance involving infidelity. It is unfortunate that most believers do not really believe in the kind of love that is dominated by the genuine good of another person.

The loving person relates equally though differently to the same sex as the opposite sex. He has enough insight into himself to understand others. He is a people person. He has sufficient respect for himself neither to exploit others nor to allow himself to be exploited in the name of love. His care for people, his interest in them, his respect for them is foremost. Anyone he deals with gets his full attention. He does not care less for his wife simply because he has another, a new focus for some of his attention. He is aware that she would not love him less for sharing herself with another. The love of such spouses is so good and great that others can be brought into their love and share their lives.

If there is one measure of the great personal relationship, the really true love, it is that it contributes to one's growth, one's stature, one's development as a human being. It never makes one less a person, more selfish, more bitter, more withdrawn, more turned in on oneself or misanthropic. It is the occasion of more and greater humanness, which shows not merely in this relationship but in all one's other relationships.

CHAPTER FIFTEEN

Married and Then Unmarried.

Extramarital love is also for those who are married and yet not married. What is the approach to loving male-female relationships in the cases of the separated, the divorced, the widow or the widower? People must love, yet they do not cease being sexual simply because they are living in the state of singleness again. For the experienced and mature there is always great opportunity for personal friendship lived well. People simply must not forget or dismiss the sexual intimacies they have rightly enjoyed and which are an integral part of their past lives. What principles are involved in their current relationships?

First of all, people in these circumstances need to be most realistic about sex. They must never dismiss it as an unimportant trifle, nor can they afford to give it an importance that it simply does not have. Sex surely is a need, a fundamental desire of the human condition. However it is by no means an indispensable need. Despite everything said by the media and the sexperts, genital sex is not a more fundamental personal need than many others which the average person lives without quite tolerably. This will indeed be denied by those for whom sex means love, companionship, excitement or security. But such people have a total misconception of sex. True, it has been implied by many social philosophers and social scientists that sex is of the essence of the human person. However, these erroneously presume that with sex goes love and many other supportive desirables that are more often missing than present in human sexual relationships. What we mean here is not doing without love, companionship, security, etc., but merely doing without genital sex, and for a very good reason. This situation is like that of people who for many reasons find it necessary or desirable to do without some things that the average, healthy person considers basic to his happiness or fulfilment. For example, a diabetic to function effectively, must handle his diabetes in an intelligent and positive way; he must accept the limitations imposed by the disease. Countless individuals have met this challenge and many others, defects or privations, despite or because of which they have risen to heights of achievement not easily equalled by most normal people. These people are realists who operate within their real rather than imagined limits, neither wasting time moaning about what is beyond them, nor dispensing themselves from obligations that are well within their capacities.

Genital sex is a human want but not a personal necessity. If it were, no normal human being could knowingly or willingly do without it. Yet many do. Tragically, few people in our affluent and permissive society have much desire to make any distinction between their needs and their wants. However, this distinction is fundamental to living lovingly, especially as a divorced or separated person, a widow or a widower. This is not merely because such people, to be moral, must do without sex. It is because many people who do need and want to love, to give and receive companionship to find the degree of security that really exists in genuine personal friendships, do not necessarily want marriage, with its obligations, and/or privileges. Many have selected a life for themselves that they are convinced they can handle and live effectively but which does not allow for actual marriage. How do these people manage?

Certainly they do not play games, say one thing when they mean another. They are honest. They know the difference between sex and love and handle sex positively. They do not pretend that it is not a part of their humanity any more than they convince themselves that life without it is impossible. A prevailing, if unfortunate, attitude to sex is either to make a mountain of it or to dismiss it as it were nothing. To many it is either a horrendous sin or the source of all fun and games. In fact, it is neither. To be sinful, sex has to be badly used, used dishonestly or improperly, in which case it is utterly destructive of good relationships. Those divorced and widowed people capable of personal loving know this. Not only have they had some experience of it but the tragic experience of many close to them has not escaped them. Dishonest sex is like stolen money. Theft of anything makes one a thief, adultery makes one an exploiter.

Being sexually hung up never saves a genuinely loving friendship for the single, divorced or bereaved person. Awareness and acceptance of the hopelessness of the sexually exploitative relationship can save whatever real love is there to be salvaged. Naive people want desperately to believe that each new experience will end differently. Most learn too late that they were being used, that they, in fact, meant nothing as people to their exploiters. The number of desperation suicides makes it painfully clear that exploitative relationships go nowhere. The wise elimination of exploiters decreases the *apparent* opportunties for friendship and love, but not the *real* ones, and does eliminate needless heartbreak. Unfortunate experience may lead to discouragement and depression, but for those willing to learn, it may well lead to a level of living which, while not highly exciting from moment to moment, is more generally satisfying than the hot and cold relationships overwhelming the ordinary person with futility and despair.

The truly loving person has such awareness of sexual exploitation that no avenue to it surprises him. This is an awareness beyond those dominated by their own satisfaction or those desperately seeking friendship. Such people have too little "other-orientation" to love. The desperate cannot afford openness in discussing the sexual dimension, for it would expose the shallowness of their motives. Yet to bypass or evade such realistic discussion is to close off a sure approach to personal love. It should be quite evident that if the sexual realities are beyond discussion, the discussion of the spiritual heights and depths of love will certainly be out of reach. There is much that is academic about love, principles that when supported by virtue, make love possible. To dismiss or avoid these principles and discussion of both sex and love makes real progress in loving impossible.

A forthrightness leading to trust always underlies the tranquillity and comfort of loving people in each other's company. Just as young married people in the early days of marriage ought to become so physically at ease with each other's bodies that they can move through the sexual more easily to personal loving, so good friends who sincerely want to be personally loving friends without getting married have to develop a physical ease with each other that can successfully negotiate normal curiosity and sexual excitement. This experience may originate in the physical care they ought to give each other in the case of older or sick people, while in younger people it may originate in the personal interest they have in each other as people, an interest that sustains physical comfort without undue sexual stimulation. With personal interest there is an absence of sexual stimulation that does not indicate boredom so much as personal acceptance. It is important to recognize that, when the personal awareness dominates, normal sexual stimulation no more carries over into irresistible genital activity than the emotion of anger carries irresistibly into violence. Loving people learn this without either the fact or the act of marriage. Anyone who does not control his sexual life will be dominated by it. There is no poorer start towards love and friendship than domination by an emotional compulsion. The genital sexual aspect of a relationship can contribute to personal loving, but it is never the basis of the loving life or relationship.

"Surely genital sex should not be given such overwhelming emphasis that two great and good friends ought not to use it in expression of their love! Surely to give it such importance one must be terribly hung up or fearful!" The response to this attitude is so simple that it is usually ignored. If sex is unimportant in friendship, then doing without it is not only possible but relatively easy. However, if it *is* important then its use or non use cannot be a matter of indifference. Surely this is what the command to avoid adultery is all about. It is God's directive not use sex as an aspect of friendship but as part of marriage. Genital sex is in no way required for loving friendship but it is for real marriage, which of course ought to involve friendship. God has revealed this simply because that is the way it works, that is the way it is. When each person in the sexual act is using that act strictly for his own pleasure or that of his partner he or she is at variance with both the nature of sex and the nature of friendship. They are using a function requiring two people, for their individual satisfaction. Those who do this make neither good friends nor good lovers. Friends or lovers not getting married must learn to live with their genital sexuality without using it, if their love and friendship are to be genuine and enduring. The rewards, to say nothing of the mutual benefits, plainly learned in the experience are worth what is involved. Love is well understood when the point is reached where one need not be ever on the alert against the intrusion of sex, or constantly apprehensive about the loss of friendship. It is precisely in these circumstances that people can associate freely and easily with personal intimacy and tranquil pleasure, (and this moreso as time elapses). In the absence of the need to dodge issues or avoid confrontation with reality, there develops great trust and a mutually healthy dependence from which comes the security of genuine love. This is the great love between two people that can be shared with still others in a most fruitful and happy manner. It is the kind of unthreatened love that everyone seeks.

Man merely *seems* to deal better with the tangibles than the intangibles, spiritual things. That is because he *feels* so much more familiar with material things; he seems more in his element. Actually he deals no better with one than the other. The spiritual is as much his element as the material. It is merely easier to measure and weigh the tangibles, which in fact, have less impact on his life than the spiritual. The mating bond does seem more real to man than the friendship bond which is so much more important, as the excruciatingly painful condition of our society reveals so clearly. True, deep friendship is what man not only wants but needs, so much more than he needs or wants sex. The attraction of young people to each other brings this out very well. Prior to marriage they feel deeply in love. Actually what they are feeling is the sexual polarity. In fact, they hardly know each other. When sexual copulation maybe minutes, days or weeks away, true friendship is generally, if not always, even years away. Previously married people of some maturity know they cannot be hurried into a real relationship. If a current one disintegrates under the pressure of reality, it is not the end of the world for them, or something they have not experienced before. The end of sexual attraction spells the end of many marriages, if not most of them. Few marriages break up between people who, over the years of marriage, became close friends. It is this second and much more human and real thing that is open to loving people who are not married and for good reasons, whatever they may be, choose not to be married. And this relationship is open to them only when, and in so far as, they can handle their sexual lives well.

A real problem seems to exist when divorced people too anxious for personal friendship and love, yet respecting a commitment to a marriage that has actually ceased to exist though still legally alive, accede to pressures to remarry. It is not too important whether these pressures are internal or external, whether from the fear of losing friendship or loneliness, from public opinion or fear of further loss of reputation. Yet is all necessarily doomed because of a second marriage? There are inescapable results. What is done is morally wrong and carries normal personal penalties, discomfort and worry. However, no one who in all honesty tries sincerely to live the truly loving life is actually penalized for doing so. The rewards far outweigh the penalties, however real. Such a person can still mature personally, can still reach true personal love, unless he or she willingly settles for less. The genuineness of the love will bring people to the point where they can and do handle the loving situation maturely and well, assuring the personal relationship by doing so. In other words, the loving experience is always a growing and maturing one. Loving is the only sure sign of personal wellbeing, wholeness. Failure in it does not make perfection impossible, merely more difficult. All roads lead to happiness for man except the willful rejection of what is right. Wrong choices lead to failure, which is remedied by right choice. When one begins all over again to love, he has made a right choice. With the new beginning comes a strength to do whatever has to be done.

When the sexual novelty, compulsion and excitement of youth persist unduly, when experience and anguish have counted for nothing one remains a perpetual juvenile. Such a one can hardly conceive of, let alone work for, the personal love available to everyone at a cost. This cost will be held reasonable, if not cheap, by those casualties of the battleground of matrimony, if they begin again to love, intent on doing a better job of it, making a more honest effort. Man must not expect instant perfection, but he must persist in his efforts towards the happiness made possible for him through his power to love.

CHAPTER SIXTEEN

The Spirituality of Sex

Man's constant preoccupation, from the earliest times, with the concept of a Supreme Being is evidence of the spiritual dimension in man. His power to believe in his fellow man whom he loves, as well as God, is again evidence of the spiritual dimension by which man contends with the things he does not know or only partially understands. This spiritual dimension is where man establishes his hierarchy of values, weighs the good and evil of his actions and makes the judgments which he calls conscience. It is the arena in which he measures his motives and contends with the imponderables of human life, where he faces the fact that he must take credit or blame for all that he thinks, says and does, which have a special significance because they are neither automatic nor inconsequential things, but human actions. In his spiritual dimension he confronts the truth and measures his actions by it: there he assents in belief and demands action on what he believes. There he decides what love is, and then loves truly and well. In the spiritual dimension man receives life's charter from God, his potential to be a thinking, loving, sexual person. The spiritual dimension is the locale of the interpersonal relationship called love.

It is in his spiritual life that man integrates sex into the spiritual experience of loving. There he comes to grips with the truth about sex, sees himself honestly in his failures. There he experiences the strong urge to be good, to be better, to love. The redemptive power of love makes itself felt in the spiritual dimension and inspires him to repent, to change for the better, to grow personally. Those who reject the spiritual dimension identify happiness with pleasure and therefore never know happiness, for pleasure as an end in itself simply does not work. Nothing is pure pleasure. Pleasure is essentially a quality of experience lived in the context of a whole life, and is helpful or harmful in so far as it contributes to or detracts from that life. Man can plainly see that his life aches with loneliness as much as his stomach aches from hunger. His minds thirsts for the spiritual as his body craves fluids. His mind and his will love as naturally as his body copulates. By nature he is a creature of the spiritual and the material worlds, equally at home in either, fully at home in neither.

The mediaeval philosophers speculated about the number of angels meeting on the point of a needle. Inflated scientists missed the point. The philosophers pondered, and tried to understand, the union of spirit and matter which they plainly saw to be a fact in man. The Latin word for spirit, soul or psyche is *anima*, which means life, animation. They wanted to know how a spiritual substance like the soul actually moved the physical body: why unhappiness could make people physically ill. Once, most diseases were considered to be purely physical but now man knows better and accepts the psychosomatic element in all his illnesses. Emotionally based illness illustrates particularly well the inseparable relationship of the spirit (psyche) to the body (soma), as man's unhappiness with himself, his conflicts and his inability to love are reflected in his body's physical malfunction.

The philosophers also knew there was a real connection between a man's genitals and his mind, his spirit. The spiritual life of man in apposition to sexual life is the life of God and grace in the human soul. But the sexual life of man essentially involves God and grace in that life and goes into the making of everything that man is, so it must add to or detract from his role as a person. Man's peace of mind, his happiness, relates directly to his harmonious sexual relations, since his sexual life is as essentially spiritual as he is. To speak of man as an angel is as ridiculous as to speak of him as a beast. Any effort to rise above sex like an angel, or copulate unthinkingly like a beast, distorts man's humanity. He may copulate piggishly, stupidly, criminally, or happily, lovingly, generously, but he always does so as a man, a human being. His basest actions have some spiritual significance because they are always reasoned or willed to some small degree, no matter how subconsciously or unwisely. Because man's sexual life always involves the choice of functioning or not functioning, it cannot be categorized as a bowel movement, as psuedo-scientists would have it. Human copulation is a matter of choice; nothing can compel a person so to function if unwilling, or restrain him if he wishes (external force left aside, of course).

The man without an arm or leg is obviously not whole; the unfeeling person is plainly not all there. Man without his spiritual dimension lacks integrity as a person. It is wrong to insist that the more spiritual a man is the less carnal he should be, for man is spirit incarnate, soul in flesh. Both his spirituality and sexuality peak in loving. Thus religious people fail when they get too bogged down in their spirituality to love; materialists fail when they get too bogged down in their sexual life to love. When sexual life is exaggerated to the detriment of the spiritual, people are unable to move through sex to personal loving. When sex becomes so formidable that it cannot be accepted as a factor in loving, people become fear-dominated, withdrawn, generally suspicious, frustrated. Married spirituality peaks when sexual intercourse is so happily integrated into the loving life that it does not distract husband or wife from their personal union, but in fact contributes to it. The time, manner and frequency of sexual intercourse is determined by love in those marriages in which spiritual values dominate, in which the personal union is deepest and most rewarding.

Sex is a matter of spiritual concern simply because it is a function worthy of man, a thoroughly human function. For this reason sex can never be simply a matter of technique or finesse but is always a vital personal matter. The spirituality of sex may be understood more clearly by considering the human hand. What is its meaning in itself and its function? One appreciates its value best by being deprived of it, for it has little value apart from the person whose hand it is. Everything that it does well or badly adds to or detracts from the person. The person can never repudiate the actions of his hand, or disclaim responsibility for what it does as if the action did not come from his mind, or the motives and meaning of the action derive from the set of values dominating his life. Certainly the hand which reaches for the privilege but rejects the obligation serves the person badly. Can less be said of the genitals?

Historically, sexual orgies have often played a major role in superstitious religious worship. To get away from this "pagan abomination", Christianity tended to downgrade sex without considering such action censorious of God, who created sex. It followed from this that chastity soon outranked charity in importance, and on this basis virginity was given a significance high above the married state without due consideration of the degree of the loving of the people involved. Sexlessness, rather than love, became the measure of holiness, and frigidity and coldness were accepted as purity and detachment. They are, in fact, sure signs of spiritual immaturity and indicate a fear-dominated, inadequate person who cannot accept sex as worthy of man, or understand love. Any one incapable of a good sexual performance is rarely if ever loving. Since such a one usually finds sex degrading, even bestial, he escapes it in a pseudospirituality buttressed by high, but false, motives. This mentality dismisses the beauty of the Song of Solomon as embarrassing. There, sensual human love is used to depict the relationship of God to the soul, in terms very understandable to the man of the times. The blushing puritan is offended by the use of such terms to describe God's purely spiritual love. While God's love for man is purely spiritual, as befits His nature, man's love for God, however spiritual, can be experienced only in the way of a male or female, as befits human nature.

Man's penchant for judging others by himself is extended even to God, whom man understandably tends to cast in his own image and likeness. It seems logical, however ridiculous, to believe that if man is a little like God then God must be a little like man. It is one thing to appreciate the inadequacy of the anthropomorphic God, another to reject God because of the inadequacy of man's understanding and terminology. It is in this vein that the command not to commit adultery seems like a censure of sex rather than God's marvellous way of telling man that his personal sexual fulfilment will be found only in the permanent commitment of a loving marriage where man's interest is in the person rather than the mere function. "Thou shalt not commit adultery" casts no aspersions on sex, which was God's idea in the first place. Nor is it God's way of taking the fun out of life. It merely insists that sex in the life of man is not the same as sex in the lives of the beasts. It is simply that man's personal happiness and fulfilment are possible only in the restriction of sexual intercourse to a person to whom he dedicates himself wholly for life. Coitus is a thing to be done only by the deeply loving man or woman. Taken out of this context, sex can have as little significance as a bowel movement. Man is made to have sexual intercourse, not as a well functioning set of genitals but as a spiritual being performing a very meaningful human act. Love lifts the act from an experience of mere pleasure to a state of happiness deriving from the relationship of the people. The place of sex in human love becomes a fact, experience, in the spiritual dimension of man.

To make sex an end in itself is to remove it from loving, to lower man's centre of gravity from his person to his sensory faculties. Man's spirituality, which integrates sex into loving, leads him into the loving union with God in heaven where sex has no place, simply because it could add nothing to the intensity of the personal union with God and others there. The spiritualization of genital sex makes man aware that his sexual life is inseparable from his loving life, and that its role is to contribute to the personal fulfilment of loving. Genital sex pleasure is mistaken for the "best there is" only by those who have not achieved the happiness of loving. The spiritual man integrates his sex into loving rather than his love into sex, as most would have it. The spiritual man also accepts that his genital, procreative function is not merely something to be played with, because in it he shares in a special way the very creativity of God.

It is precisely the man with a healthy spiritual life who can relinquish life itself, let alone its attractive pleasures, for a principle in which he believes, or for a fellow man he loves. He has the virtue, that is, the power to do what ought to be done, in sexual matters, as in all things involved in personal fulfilment. He can engage in or refrain from sexual intercourse simply because he loves. Man's sex life can be dominated by many factors, but it is when those factors are standards beyond the material, a true set of values, that sex does contribute to the happiness of the person. Under the spiritual influence of love, sexual intercourse is purposefully performed with real happiness and joy.

Scientific studies of sexual intercourse lose their validity primarily because they discount, or ignore entirely, the spiritual dimension essentially present in all human behaviour, being content to investigate sex on a purely mechanistic or technical basis isolated from all that a man is. Regardless of his feelings, man simply cannot slough off the spiritual significance of his sexual life. His earthiest actions are dominated by a hierarchy of values which, to be genuine, must represent the world of the spirit. Hungry men can fast for a worthy cause as married people or celibates can refrain from sexual intercourse for a reason. Surely to be of loving service to the people of God is ample reason for celibates to refrain from sexual intercourse for life.

Man's children can be born through love, lust or indifference, by design or by accident. Man can get rid of undesirables by abortion or breed bodies to supply organ transplants for privileged or important citizens. But whatever he chooses to do, he cannot escape the consequences of his actions nor repudiate the world of his options. It is absolutely ridiculous to think that the use of his genitals can rightly be capricious or irresponsible, or dominated by his feelings of the moment, completely out of the context of reality. Unless the genitals are used in conformity with a set of standards including the spiritual motivations and sanctions open to him, values which are moral as well as material, the result will inevitably be personally and socially monstrous. It is surely reasonable to consider that man is made to do his own thing, but that thing is what he is made for rather than merely what he feels at the moment.

It is thoroughly regrettable that the expression "to turn on" is generally restricted to emotional excitement. It describes beautifully the spiritual power of the loving person to enkindle others, brighten their lives, evoke warm tenderness and deep love. The spiritual dimension's relationship to sex consists in its power to direct sex into acute awareness of others and active interest in them, not as bodies but as people. Surely the union of two people in a common, worthy cause is much deeper, more fully human than the union of a man and woman in the exclusively sexual embrace. It is a fundamental frustration of marriage that the sexual embrace in itself does not bring the people, but merely the bodies, closer. Love and understanding unite people more closely than sex ever can. Yet only God and man have a deeper union than the husband and wife whose sexual embrace is but the beginning of a personal intermingling far surpassing the actual limitations of pure sex.

Sexual reactions to people are normal steps in the discovery of personal beauty, truth and goodness, things deeply esteemed because of the spiritual dimension. If a consequent relationship involves the total sexual giving to each other in love, it is because the person-to-person interest, understanding and love made it possible. Lacking spiritual depth and high human values, many naively see a meaning and promise in the precipitate sexual adventure which is not really there. Such an eventuality is avoided by sufficient spiritualization of sex to move from mere sexual reaction to attention to the whole person. Into such love sex can be happily integrated. Thus love is the real wonder of man. It is plainly the image of God in man, the Spirit of God among men. It gives Christianity its real meaning, and the role of sex in such a religion is plainly obvious. Sex reaches its spiritual zenith in such love, as it does its highest pleasure. But actually human sex on any other basis ultimately disappoints.

CHAPTER SEVENTEEN

Sex Hangups

"Hangup" seems to be the term hung on anyone whose attitude to something does not meet with general acceptance. Thus a "sex hangup" can mean the attitude of anyone who rejects a purely hedonistic, pleasure-dominated, irresponsible capacity to copulate promiscuously. It seems more valid to consider a sex hangup to refer to the attitude of those who deprive sex of its specifically human significance and reduce it to a lesser role than it must play in the personal growth and maturity of man.

In this sense there is no greater sex hangup than the current prostitution of sex to man's greed for wealth, and, of course, the power that flows from that wealth. The very word "prostitution" indicates a hangup. It refers to the abuse of something good for venal purposes at odds with the very purpose for which that good thing is meant. For that very reason prostitution in common usage is applied to the activities of the woman or man who makes her or his body available for financial gain. And what more convincing evidence of current sex hangups by professedly liberated people than the general utilization of every aspect of sex for commercial advertising. Sex today is indeed big business, managed on as efficient a basis as any other highly developed business enterprise. Not only is flesh directly involved, but technology is made to serve in peddling it. The creative arts of writing, painting, drama, photography, filming, advertising, all address themselves to exploiting the human libido for the financial gain of the entrepreneurs. Pornography has been industrialized through the publishing business, and has been protected in the process by governments, both legally and through bribery and corruption, safeguarded by great legal minds either prostituted directly to sexploitation, or so blinded by pride or arrogance as to consider themselves the protectors of public licence. It is incredible that the legal and academic worlds find themselves incapable of defining obscenity, despite all educational advances. Indeed, academic progress does seem retrogression, in that the more ideas man comes up with the more difficult he finds it to express himself clearly enough to be understood correctly. Actual sex hangups have their bases in those attitudes that so twist sex as to make it the master rather than the servant of man.

The current sex hangup is the general unwillingness or inability to accept sex as an important but limited human function—that is, to accept that it can never be an end in itself. It is this hangup that has allowed sex to become the tremendous rip-off it is in our culture. It matters little that this hangup derives to some extent from the inhibited approach to sex that until recently has prevailed in Western culture, as evidenced in the puritanical, Victorian, rigid sexual ethic. However, the permissive cure for this problem is more and more obviously worse than the disease.

A nearly universal sex hangup is the identification of love with sex and/or marriage. A noisy, well-publicized, if small segment of society has tried to cure this hangup by recommending liberation through free sex and open marriage. As expected, such a simplistic approach to so real a problem leads only to more confusion and deeper, more ingrained hangups. It would take a truly scientific (in the best sense of the word) depth study of Western Christian history, culture and religion to trace the basis for this identification. In non-Western, non-Christian societies and cultures and in most primitive civilizations there does not seem to have been this close link between love, sex and marriage. The very concept of relating love to sex or marriage would utterly bewilder primitive people. Does this link indicate that progress has been made, or that somewhere along the line progress went off the track?

Primitive people accepted that sex was the function through which children were born. Children were a social necessity for defence, production and progress. Our technology seems to have made them expendable or surplus in this regard. That our society has so quickly and definitely declared them completely unnecessary for "the quality of life" is dangerous thinking indeed. In earlier times marriage seemed an effort to so regulate the function of sex that progress in civilization could be assured by strong family ties. In the unlikely assumption that this necessity has already been achieved and secured, marriage might well be obsolete. However, the degree of emotional immaturity everywhere evident in our society hardly warrants declaring marriage meaningless as of now. In fact the sexual and/or married lives of people are an excellent barometer of the degree of loving of the people living them. The progress of our world actually depends on just how loving or unloving those people are. People as obviously interested as most moderns are in more sex and less marriage have a long way to go before they contribute much meaning to the quality of life.

A tragic consequence of identifying love with sex and/or marriage is that when married people discover that their sexual and married lives have not automatically become loving, they are shocked and disappointed. They had been led to expect otherwise. Yet this discovery could be most beneficial if they used it as the occasion to begin to learn to love. They would then see how their love does automatically flow into their sexual and married lives. They would recognize the difference in those lives because of the incipient love. But when, on the contrary, disappointed and hurt, they back away from the unloving sexual-married life only to look around desperately for some other loser with whom to begin the same process all over again, it is very unlikely that the second relationship will be any different from the first. True, it has become fashionable for such people to seek marriage counseling before the final dissolution of their marriages. It is even legally mandatory in many places to do so. When, unhappily, the marriage counselors have the same false notions about sex and marriage, no one is helped, and, in fact, the problems are compounded.

However real the minor benefits of permissiveness, the litany of failures directly attributed to it seems endless. Permissiveness has exposed some serious errors in teaching methodology, but it is not conducive to love, which requires strong self-discipline. Well-meaning parents, aided and abetted by the paternalism of the Church, tended to take liberty from their children "for their own good". Yet liberty is God's expressed trust in man to do his thing and, with God's help, to do it well. Liberty is certainly the fundamental condition for loving, which is the "thing" for which man was created. However wrong the reasons, permissiveness has restored some of the liberty taken away by overprotective parents "for the good of their children". The failure of permissiveness has made it abundantly clear that sex is not love, that sex is no promised land of unlimited pleasure and joy. Since permissiveness has made sex a subject for free discussion with anyone, at any time, in any place, people are getting more opportunity to learn the true limits of sex. However, through permissiveness, the social scientists and behaviourists who undertook the liberation of the world from its sex hangups have led people into worse hangups than the ones from which they were to be liberated. They have made sex an end in itself that leads to reality and disappointment. If people are now much more prepared and even anxious to look deeper for the love which alone makes human relationships meaningful, the experience may not be wasted. They may learn that the narrow limits of sexual pleasure can be extended and made wider by man's power to love, which finds in sexual expression only one of its outlets.

Two prevalent attitudes underlie countless sex hangups. The first is acceptance of the reality of the genitals but either failure to consider or refusal to accept that with the equipment comes the urge to use it. Thus, for any number of reasons—ignorance, fear, cultural or religious misconceptions—many willingly or even gladly suppress the desires inseparable from the genital fact. They deny the genitals the normal attention necessarily or even gladly given other organs or functions of their bodies. Such people manage to live as if they were neuter gender, penalizing themselves into a state something between confusion and complete inability to cope. Many of these people consider that in repressing the sexual emotions they achieve something great. They dispose of a vexatious problem that many people handle badly, and do it rather easily. They have no sense of mutilating themselves by psychological surgery. They ignore an important area of their humanity without a backward glance, hardly suspecting the bleak future they have created for themselves.

A second attitude to sex provides any number of hangups: that with the genitals comes undeniably the urge to use them, which urge is normal, natural, healthy, (which it surely is) but that that urge must admit of no restriction or direction. Sex is a source of pleasure and comfort to be used whenever and however one's feelings indicate. Despite there being obviously nothing in life that can be used on these terms, many consider that sex should admit of no restraint other than what is criminal or personally unacceptable.

This latter is the curious attitude of those people defending ecology and protesting pollution as if pornography (especially for personal gain) was not pollution, apparently quite unaware that pollution of the mind is much more calamitous than pollution of the atmosphere. There is simply no human pursuit that can admit of no restraint, even for one's own sake, if not for the sake of society. There are very real limits to eating, drinking, working, playing, making money, striving for political office or power. There is a point in every pursuit beyond which one has too much of a good thing. Uninhibited sex is no better or worse than uninhibited anything else. There must come a time when every man recognizes excess of pleasure by the physical or emotional pain experienced through it. That point is reached when any appetite or function works against the overall purpose of man to be a thinking, loving human being.

Man's denial of, or failure to recognize sin leads inevitably to domination of his purpose as man by some lesser appetite which enslaves him. However faulty the teaching of religion or presentation of moral strictures may have been, because of human limitations, it is ridiculous to attribute every kind of sexual hangup to guilt complexes flowing from erroneous religious concepts. Certainly the ego-inflated social philosophers, deluded by the impressive, if limited, achievements of man, and, presuming for man a creativity rightly God's alone, have messed up things quite seriously by rejection of the reality of sin. Such people are as religiously naive as they claim religious people to be scientifically naive. The most fundamental concepts of God would make it plain that the Creator of life alone knows what works and what does not. Therefore to follow that Creator's directives is to live well, to reject his directives is to fail. By sin man does reject God, but more to the point he surely wrecks himself. Man looks a little ridiculous when he considers sin something created by God rather than committed by man. Surely sin, rather than God or religion (man's relationship to God), is responsible for man's guilt complexes. Sin is a deliberate wrongdoing by man, for which he has genuine guilt and suffers inescapable consequences. Man's guilt complexes arise from his fruitless effort to have his cake and eat it too. He wants to do as he pleases while being dispensed from the consequences. Every guilt complex covers serious dishonesty, rather than mere honest error.

Sex like everything created by God, is good. But like the products of General Motors or any other efficiently run commerical enterprise, sex comes with a clear set of directions. It works best when handled by competent people under the right conditions in a positive and respectful way. No company stands behind its guarantee if the conditions set out in its operational manuals are not followed. Sex, too, has conditions inseparable from its functional use if happy consequences are to result. These conditions are as physical, emotional, psychological and spiritual, as is man. Yet even bright people who flagrantly abuse sex wonder why it leads to misery, rather than happiness. Only when human sex does express, as it can, true love, does it expand the narrow pleasure limits of the genitals into personal joy.

Sexual sin is the exclusive use of sex for man's personal pleasure rather than for the purpose for which the equipment was designed. Since that equipment is fashioned to couple complementarily with that of another human being, to be truly human sex must be part of a personal relationship, that is, it must fit in with the overall purpose of both people, which is to be loving. However great sexual pleasure, sex is not purely or primarily for pleasure. In fact, the highest possible degree of pleasure comes from its fundamental and respectful use, in love. That is precisely what expands the narrow pleasure of genital sex into the joy of loving.

Those who insist on identifying happiness with pleasure can only learn how wrong they are through the improper use of sex. Whenever man uses anything the wrong way, however innocent or honest his error, he discovers his mistakes in disappointment. Surely sex ought to be used with at least the same care and respect as any irreplaceable piece of essential equipment. Such care would bring the same result, a sense of reverence incompatible with sex hangups or guilt complexes.

Most sex hangups are traceable to some emotional disorder, to some way in which a person's feelings dominate judgement, positively or negatively. Impotence is a problem to many men, and increasingly so in an age when one's manhood is being gauged by bedroom prowess. When man's sexual appetites are being hailed as so strong and unmanageable, curiously enough, impotence remains a tribute to the potency of fear, which can make an erection, a rather simple and undemanding achievement in normal circumstances, an impossibility. The proliferating sex clinics, most of which are admittedly phoney fronts for making money through sexual exploitation, are trying to teach man to so reduce his fear that he can finally achieve an erection and have intercourse, however unsatisfactorily. Such a thing is hardly a challenge at all for a chimpanzee.

Surely if the obvious were admitted, that sexual vigour is not the criteria for manhood, the hangups underlying sexual impotence would quickly disappear. When fear so dominates that the libido cannot break through, one is not dominated by love, or a concern for another. Sexual impotence is extremely rare in the truly loving person.

Sexual impotence and premature ejaculation are two major problems in the trade of the sexperts "teaching" males to copulate. The first concerns those people driven to fantasy because in the real world their libido is dominated by fear. The latter, rather patronizingly referred to as "hit-and-run" drivers, are so dominated by any sexual stimulus that the libido obliterates all awareness of their partner, making them highly unsatisfactory lovers. The sexual act with them is devoid of love. It is a self-satisfying, egocentric performance, always exploitative, never loving. Obviously to them, loving means even less than copulation. Surely love, which diminishes the former's fears and the latter's lust cures these problems. In both cases it is the function of loving rather than the sexual function that is at fault.

Pride, lust, greed are among the seven sins well called *capital*, for from these sins flow all hangups. In all cases man is hung up on himself. He makes himself the centre of the universe; he wants to run his world his own way. This state is in contradiction to love, which alone liberates man from his ego and hang ups. Love is "other-oriented". Where is the truly loving person with sex hangups? Where is the egomaniac without them?

Unfortunately, in the misguided world of academe, sex ought to be better understood and lived with. This cannot be so unless sexual morality is well taught and highly respected. True sexual morality cures sex hangups, for it ties sex into the power to love where it is properly directed. As in all other aspects of human living, when sex is handled badly there is a penalty to be paid. It is often the complications of sexual abuse that prevent man's development into a loving person, leaving him more hungup, with diminished potential for happiness.

Sexually hung up people tend to categorize sex as the most dreadful of horrors or the sublimest of delights, when in reality it is neither. If it were, as so many insist, an essentially pleasure-giving experience, there would not be so many people insisting that it does nothing for them. Impotence in men and frigidity in women would be rarer than they are. Sex can be a horror or a delight depending on many factors but primarily on its meaning in the relationship of the people involved. There is a very straight, physical pleasure to sex when enjoyed by people quite content to keep it on a purely physical or animal level. Then it has maximal pleasure but minimal personal meaning. It has nowhere to go from the physical. But when the personal element is high, that is, when love is real, there is a tender fulfilment experienced by the two people expressing something very personal and precious to each other. However, with this purely physical act of intercourse there can well be hate expressed in a frightening violence. *Rapists* are obviously so sick that they get venereal delight not from their libido but from the vindictive violence of their action. They are apparently incapable of expressing love, being so dominated by hate and contempt. Serious emotional illness underlies the sexual hangups of such people.

Sexual abuse manifests sickness in the same way as does abuse of drugs, food, work, and many other things. Pleasure is a factor of human life, but the inordinate pursuit of pleasure to the detriment of others shows an irresponsibility quite at odds with the power to love. Exploiters invite exploitation in return and despise themselves for doing so. They have as little respect for themselves as they have for the exploited. Every exploitation is an evidence of some serious hang up. Unless one has respect for himself, sooner or later he takes his frustrations out on those to whom he is attracted and so *feels* he must dominate, or on those he *feels* have rejected him and therefore must be punished by him. In such serious sickness it is not another person but society itself that must feel his hate and be punished. Too few recognize, in the many examples we have of one man's war on society, the manifestation of emotional illness often originating in sex hangups.

The homosexual phenomenon represents a special sex hangup. It is so normal to relate to the opposite sex through the inherent sexual polarity that something has obviously happened to those who do not. People who do not experience sexual polarity are like those who do not get warm in the sun. They are either withdrawn or inhibited to an alarming degree. Many of them experienced childhood sexploitation. Many have experienced domination by the parent of the opposite sex to the degree that they have identified with that parent. Such strong identification neutralized the sexual polarity, leaving them with an attraction to the same sex. The phenomenon is complex, the cure difficult. However, there is no cure at all when people neither see the sickness nor the need for help. "Gay" society considers even the desire for help as disloyal to "their own". "Gay" people want what no one can have, life on their own terms. They demand that society accommodate itself to them. Thus they compound a sick person and a sick situation into an impossibility. Suicide or some bizarre manifestation of defiance often ensues. The average homosexual generally conforms resentfully to straight society.

There is a good deal of ever available and accessible pleasure from one's own genitals. Sex, however, essentially involves two people and society. By oneself, and in itself, sex has little human significance other than self-indulgent pleasure or emotional pleasure compensation for the lack of personal happiness. Certainly solitary genital activity has no relationship to love. Whether it is masturbation, fantasizing, voyeurism, exhibitionism or whatever, it is an abuse. It carries an unacceptable penalty to the personal maturing process. It indicates either an unwillingness or inability to cope with reality. Real life presents many avenues to satisfaction to the ordinary person. To seek physical pleasure in one's own body through sexual arousal indicates bankruptcy in the emotional fulfilment department of life. Autoeroticism is typical of the withdrawn loner fearful of rejection, overwhelmed by feelings of inadequacy or worthlessness.

Everyone has hangups. That they should exist in the sexual field only reflects the humanity of man's sexual life. The important thing is to be aware of them in one's own life and be prepared to deal with them as sanely and maturely as possible. None of them need be fatal. Open discussion of them can be helpful if it does not degenerate into navel-gazing, self-pity or exhibitionism. Every obstacle to loving that is effectively dealt with, overcome or removed makes life more meaningful and rewarding. With the obstacles removed, the garbage out of his life, man finds himself functioning well, loving and fulfilled.

Conclusion: The Personal Fitness of Man

Enjoying leisure, comfort, pleasure and entertainment on a hitherto unknown scale, man still finds personal happiness remarkably rare. He is surprised by his general reaction to affluence—it is not gratitude but greed. Hunger, poverty, sickness and other basic ills are rather easy to contend with; man, however, is not. He is still the problem.

The shrill protests of ecologists and conservationists hardly veil the fact that pollution is not the work of factories but of people, that it is not smoke but selfishness that threatens the balance of nature. It is ridiculous to think of overpopulation as the world's primary problem. It is, in fact, the underpopulation of the world by loving and concerned people. When man cleans up himself, he will have made a fine beginning to cleaning up his world.

Apart from the churches there are many worthy organizations appealing for man's attention to his condition, welfare and reform. His abuse of alcohol and other drugs, his heavy smoking, overeating, frenetic activism, his innumerable other vices are all held up to him for his immediate concern. Many respond to these public and private pleas positively with modest acceptance of certain amounts of discipline. But most people evade the issue simply because they need virtue, and that is a word they do not much like. It seems to threaten the freedom clung to so desperately by those who insist on living as they please rather than as they should. But surely most people who do admit the need for physical fitness must at least suspect the even greater need for personal fitness, for a concerted effort to be real human beings, to love.

Man must learn to love. He must see and admit that sex is not love and too seldom has anything to do with love. He must also admit that while there is nothing anti-love about marriage, neither is there anything about it that is essentially loving. Love is not something one falls into naturally, effortlessly, but something achieved with years of learning and practice. Painfully acquired discipline, like patience, always precedes the love that reaches perfection in single life, marriage or celibacy.

Whatever helps one to love is good; whatever retards the development of the loving person is destructive and bad. Since the perfection of man is love, it requires his best efforts; it ought to be his main thrust in life. Man is proud; he is selfish, lustful, greedy and dishonest. His redemption is achieved through the loving in his life. This is what God achieves when man allows Him into his life. Love is the presence of God in the life of a man.

When man is no longer dominated by his urge to suck pleasure from the breast of affluence without making a spiritual return for his joy, there is love in his life. Man's return to the world for its investment in him will be spiritual when he accepts that love must do more than tickle his palate, stimulate his venereal nerves, fill his eye with beauty or his head with glory. Then he understands by personal experience that love lays open the very core of man from which his happiness flows. When genuinely loving man has fully evolved, he has become everything he could ever hope to be. He is fully human, he is happy, he is at peace with himself.